Thoughts From the Greeks

THOUGHTS FROM THE GREEKS

PRESTON H. EPPS

UNIVERSITY OF MISSOURI PRESS
COLUMBIA, MISSOURI

Standard Book Number 8262–0082–6
Library of Congress Card Number 70–99909
Manufactured in the United States of America
Copyright © 1969 by the Curators of the University of Missouri
All Rights Reserved

Foreword

I have frequently been asked what on earth I found in Greek literature that would justify the time and effort required to become acquainted with the Greek language. I decided therefore to list and comment briefly on some of the surprising and helpful ideas I have found well thought out and expressed by the Greek writers. It occurred to me that in this way I might also pay some small tribute to the help I have received from a lifetime study devoted to this subject. For the numerous basic ideas I found conceived, formulated, and sanely discussed in Greek literature have proved of immense help to me as I have tried to come to terms, as intelligently and constructively as possible, with the life I had been given the privilege of living and the world I had to live it in. And to be able to contemplate these ideas directly, as they were originally expressed, rather than through some translation colored, if not really modified, by the translator's predilections—as translations always are—has afforded me more satisfaction than most people would imagine. For a translation can often mislead as well as lead.

One should notice that it is the permanent or universal ideas thought out and expressed by the Greeks, rather than their marvelous statues, temples, and art, that most interest me. By this, I do not mean to scorn in any way such concrete accomplishments of the Greeks.

They are simply of less importance *to me* than the basic ideas developed by the Greeks. In passing judgment, therefore, on what is to follow, one will need to remember this predilection of mine, if one is to judge it most fairly.

There are two other things to be kept in mind:

The Greeks I shall be quoting and referring to were not average, ordinary Greeks any more than our thinkers are average Americans. The Greeks I shall be mentioning were the superior and more daring Greek thinkers. The average Greek seems to have been as ordinary as the generality of men are everywhere.

The second thing to remember is that these ideas were arrived at and expressed by the Greeks, not in the light of what is known today, but in the light only of what was known some 2500 years ago. It is difficult to keep this in mind in any meaningful way and is even impossible to realize it fully and perfectly. Yet readers must remember the period in history in which these ideas were thought out and expressed, if they are to evaluate them fairly and understand them best.

I hope, finally, that the following discussions will be considered only for what they really are meant to be—one professor's valedictory to forty-five years of as happy and rewarding associations and experiences as any professor ever had. Except for the final item, the ideas presented here have all been selected from passages in Greek literature prior to 323 B.C. Even though comments and interpretations of various scholars and commentators have been omitted, the conclusions presented were arrived at only after years of reading, study, and investigation into the critical literature concerning these ideas and Greek literature in general. Also, very little in the way of parallel ideas in earlier or later cultures has been brought in. The reason for this has been that, in the case of presentations intended more as a tribute to Greek thinking ability and achievement than as any contribution to these, neither of the categories omitted seemed necessary. I trust that readers will keep all this in mind.

I wish to express herewith my thanks and gratitude: to Mr. Virgil Markham for permission to use the quotation from his father's "Man-Test"; to Harper & Row for permission to use, from *Greek Literature in Translation*, parts of "Faction in Greece" by Thucydides, "One's Duty and Tacit Contract with One's Country," "The Death of Socrates" by Plato, and Cleanthes' "Hymn to Zeus."

PRESTON H. EPPS

CHAPEL HILL, NORTH CAROLINA
July, 1969

Contents

By each of us there stands straightway from birth
A kindly spirit-guide to lead us through
The labyrinthine mysteries of life.

And we must never think this spirit evil,
Nor fraught with wickedness to harm our lives,
But always hold God good in everything.

Those who themselves turn base in character
And complicate their lives exceedingly,
When they have ruined all through heedlessness,
Declare and hold as cause this spirit-guide,
And make him evil, becoming such themselves.

MENANDER, Frag. 549K

I The Futility of Unyielding Anger

Our first idea to be taken up is also the earliest. It is found in the eighteenth book of the *Iliad*, lines 107–111, where Homer recounts Achilles' apparent recognition that his hasty and stubborn anger has been the indirect cause of the death of his dearest friend. His agonizing words, translated, are these:

> How I wish that strife, both that from gods and that which comes from men, would perish utterly! And also anger which incites to rage even those exceedingly wise—anger which builds, like smoke, within men's breasts till it grows sweeter than trickling honey! Such anger did Agamemnon, lord of men, lately provoke in me.

Here we meet the earliest intimation I know of in Western literature concerning the futility of passionate anger. Such anger generally cancels out an individual's reasoning powers, except those which will aid him in venting his raging anger as he wishes. It also frequently boomerangs on him in disappointing ways. Achilles' conduct and the consequences here facing him are Homer's example of how unreasoning anger can frequently recoil on the one who yields to it. Let me review for you the background of Achilles' tragic situation.

As you will remember, the custom in ancient wars was for the victors to kill the men, except priests, and put the women up as prizes for the generalissimo and the principal fighters. The Greeks had captured Chryse, a region near Troy, where a priest of Apollo named Chryses lived with his daughter Chryseïs. Agamemnon had been awarded Chryseïs as his meed of honor, while Achilles received as his prize a maid named Briseïs.

Sometime later the priest Chryses came and begged Agamemnon to return his daughter, only to be ordered rudely away. In answer to the priest's prayers, Apollo soon sent such a death-dealing plague on the Greek army that the pyres of the dead were ever ablaze, according to Homer.

In the face of the continuing plague, Achilles suggested that the Greeks consult a soothsayer to discover the reason for Apollo's anger. In reply to their entreaties, the soothsayer declared that the plague was sent because Agamemnon had refused to release the daughter of the priest Chryses and that the plague would continue until Apollo was appeased by her release.

Having little choice, Agamemnon angrily consented to return Chryseïs, but apparently blamed Achilles for his having to give her up. He therefore declared he would take Briseïs, Achilles' prize of honor, for himself. The enraged Achilles, vowing he would never fight again for the Greeks, promptly withdrew from the army.

Inasmuch as Agamemnon still continued unsuccessful in the war, he in time repented of his anger and sought Achilles' forgiveness and his assistance in battle. Envoys were sent to Achilles offering to return Achilles' prize of honor, Briseïs—whom Agamemnon had not touched—plus a list of gifts that requires some thirty-three lines of Greek to enumerate. By any measure, Agamemnon went far more than "the second mile" in his efforts to make amends to Achilles. But, despite the lavish and extensive gifts of reconciliation, Achilles remained adamant and made short shrift of Agamemnon's offer.

As the Greeks became more and more hard pressed by Hector and the Trojans, Achilles' bosom friend Patroclus asked Achilles to permit him to wear Achilles' divinely-bestowed armor into battle. Achilles consented, but warned Patroclus to avoid combat with Hector, the mightiest of the Trojan warriors. But the temptation was apparently too great both for Patroclus and for Hector, and Patroclus died at Hector's hand. As was the custom, the victorious Hector stripped the dead Patroclus of Achilles' special armor.

As a consequence, then, of his stubborn and unreasoning anger, Achilles thus lost his two most treasured possessions: his divinely-bestowed armor and his dearest friend. The twin blows to Achilles were calamitous, considering the transcendent importance such armor held for a warrior hero, and what friendship could mean to early men, especially when they and their friends were conjoined in common dangers. Remember also that this particular friendship between Achilles and Patroclus was so strong and close that it has become one of the more famous friendships in literature.

With his special armor and his dearest friend both irretrievably lost, Achilles seems, according to the passage from Homer quoted above, to have been brought to see clearly the futility of unreasoning anger.

Whether Achilles had had other angry actions boomerang on him, I do not know. But with this one at least he seems to have realized with a new understanding that unreasoning anger, like revenge, promises a sweet fulfillment which it seldom, if ever, gives. More often than not its fulfillment, in the end, "bites like a serpent and stings like an adder," as the Scripture says.

And this seems quite natural; for a person caught up in unreasoning anger has temporarily canceled out all his reasoning powers except those that will aid and abet him in accomplishing his angry purpose. This, I suppose, is why persons seldom act wisely or even sensibly when they are inordinately angry. Those who are not given to inordinate anger may well feel that the wish and observation of Achilles are not worth this discussion; but to those addicted to this human failing, his statement can have much to say.

The joker in this discussion is the word *anger*, since it is used at times instead of indignation, again to mean genuine anger, and finally to mean raging anger. Our understanding of the term is further confused by the misuse some psychologists make of the word. How often one hears that an addiction to anger is indispensable if one is to be as spirited as a normally healthful person should be. Were *indignation* substituted for *anger*, the statement would be more nearly accurate and more acceptable to thinking men.

But when does indignation become anger and when does it become raging anger? The following distinctions have helped me with this problem:

4

Indignation remains indignation, even though it may be quite vehement, as long as it is definitely under the control of the rational processes. There is nothing timid or weak about genuine indignation. It can be just as firm and just as insistent as genuine anger that its demands be satisfied. *But so long as it remains under the control of the mind it is still indignation and not anger.*

But indignation is transmuted into unreasoning anger once the mind so capitulates to the emotional feelings aroused by indignation that it is no longer a true adviser. In its surrender, it becomes only an obsequious lackey to encourage, justify, and execute any act the unreasoning feelings may at the time prompt.

When the unreasonably angry individual finally strikes out with sinister intent, by words or acts, at the object of his anger, his unreasoning anger is transmuted thereby into what may be described as raging anger. Such a conception of indignation as that given above and such a valid distinction, as I see it, between indignation and the two types of anger have given me what has proved to be a most satisfactory perspective on this subject.

Whenever the Greeks attended either of Sophocles' plays concerned with Oedipus, king of Thebes, they must have realized what havoc and suffering could be worked in human life and affairs by a quickness to irrational anger and suspicion. For, as Sophocles portrays Oedipus in these two plays, *quickness to unreasoning anger and suspicion was the character flaw that betrayed him into his horrible plight.* Sophocles' interest in this flaw was such that he strung words for anger and angry passion like a scarlet thread throughout both plays, resorting to them more than twenty times.

Even Oedipus' most loving daughter Antigone suggests (O.C.1195–8) that reflection on his past sufferings would show "what evil ends follow from unreasoning anger." And Creon, his kinsman and successor at Thebes, reminds Oedipus a bit earlier (O.C.854) that his anger, always his undoing, has again been given rein. If he had restrained his anger when the boor in Corinth taunted him with being a supposititious child, Oedipus would not have gone to consult Delphi in the matter. And had he yielded the right of way to King Laius and his retinue (as was customary) instead of angrily and violently resisting demands to give way, he would almost certainly never have killed the King, who happened to be his father. And finally, if he had not gone into a rage when he discovered the truth about himself, he would not have irrationally blinded himself.

The tragedy of Achilles and that of Oedipus have helped me to see with convincing clarity that indignation is a sound, healthy, and adequate reaction to any wrong, whereas that which is real anger is not. For indignation, however vehement and insistent, stays always under the control of the mind, whereas anger and rage do not. For such a clear, helpful insight and distinction I shall always be grateful. This understanding has been of immense aid to me in coming to livable terms with this seemingly intractable human feeling.

II The Effects of Voluntary Acts Are Inescapable

We come now to a second helpful insight that came to me from the Greeks. As far as I know, this perception is not explicitly stated in the Greek, but stems from my interpretation of two separate ideas emphasized by Socrates in two of the Platonic dialogues.

The dialogue was a unique literary invention of the Greeks, brought to its fullest and maturest development by Plato, thirty-five of whose dialogues survive. Since Socrates is the chief spokesman in all but one of these dialogues, they are occasionally referred to as Socratic dialogues. They illustrate fully what has come to be known as the Socratic method, which continually involved the "pupils" or respondents (generally one at a time) in the discussion. Socrates will not pass from one point to another until his interlocutor admits he understands what is being said. The meticulous details Socrates will insist on going through to be sure that his respondent comprehends each step in the presentation make these dialogues tedious at times and thus objectionable to modern readers. But the dialogues repay well those who have the patience to read them; I don't know any literature, except the Bible, that is more replete with rich and noble moral and ethical ideas and inspiration.

Moreover, the ideas of the dialogues are rationally

presented from knowledge up rather than primarily from preconception down, as biblical morality generally is. (As I taught in these dialogues, I had the great good fortune also of taking students through a large part of the New Testament Gospel material each year for thirty years. And to see how often ideas from the Greeks complemented rationally some of those in the gospels was one of the most rewarding experiences of my professorial life.) Any reader desiring to see a brief, though hardly typical example of these Platonic-Socratic dialogues can do so by turning to pages 140–50.

But let's turn now to the subject of this chapter. Stated in modern terms, it is this: The innermost self and character of every man is inescapably affected by his every *voluntary act and freely adopted purpose or attitude.*

This means that every voluntary act and purpose, consummated by anyone, augments and makes more regnant in that person's life and conduct whatever store of feeling he may already possess in the depth of his innermost self that is akin to the deed or purpose being consummated by him. Stated more specifically, every deed or purpose emanating from ill will, vindictiveness, malice, or man's inhumanity to man that is voluntarily effected by the individual always increases and reinforces whatever tendencies and urges he already has to ill will, malice, vindictiveness, and the like. The effect on the doer is automatic and unfailing.

By the same logic, every voluntary deed or purpose actuated and accomplished by anyone out of creative good will, generosity, or affectionate regard automatically increases and further invigorates, in the same way and to the same extent, whatever fund of these and similar feelings the person may already have stored in his innermost self. Here again the effect on the doer is instantaneous and unfailing.

The two instances in the dialogues from which this perception has been derived are these: Socrates quite directly in the *Gorgias* and indirectly in the *Crito* argues that, if the choice should become necessary, he would always prefer *to be treated unjustly* rather than treat anyone unjustly. In his discussion with the youthful Polus (*Gorgias* 469b-c), we encounter this exchange:

SOCRATES.
To act unjustly happens to be the greatest of evils.
POLUS.
Isn't it a greater evil to be treated unjustly?
SOCRATES.
Not at all.
POLUS.
You mean you would prefer to be treated unjustly than to treat another unjustly?
SOCRATES.
I wouldn't prefer either; but if it should become necessary for me either to treat someone unjustly or be treated unjustly, I would choose *to be treated unjustly* rather than to treat anyone unjustly.

That seems about as explicit as it could be. Of the same, though less direct, tenor are the two reasons Socrates gives Crito as to why he cannot retaliate against his native Athens in return for the wrong she had done him. He reminds Crito (sec. 49b & c) that "to act unjustly is in all cases both an evil and a shameful thing for the person doing it. . . . Therefore one must never do evil to anyone, nor must one ever return evil for evil, no matter to what extent he has been wronged by anyone."

The mental framework back of these statements seems to be represented in the following syllogistic conclusion arrived at by Socrates:

1. Every unjust act voluntarily done by anyone always leaves some trace of itself in the "soul" (we would say innermost depths) of the doer.
2a. Even though *to be treated unjustly* is always an evil, such treatment does not *automatically* leave any trace (scar) of evil in the "soul" of the one so treated.
  b. But *to treat one unjustly* is a greater evil, since such treatment always *automatically* leaves some trace (scar) of itself in the "soul" of the one committing the injustice.
3. Of the two evils therefore, it is better for one *to be treated unjustly* than for him *to treat another unjustly*.

So, since Socrates wanted to keep his "soul" as free as possible of evil, whenever he was forced to choose he always chose to be treated unjustly rather than treat another unjustly.

The second idea from which the interpretation here presented has come is found in the myth near the close of the *Gorgias*. To summarize: Socrates declares to the recalcitrant Callicles in this myth (*Gorgias* 524 ff.):

Just as in the case of the human body, Callicles, the entire nature of the soul, plus all that it has suffered through the various practices and pursuits of its possessor, stands out quite clearly, once the soul has been stripped of its bodily covering. When therefore the souls of men come before the judge [in Hades], . . . he frequently sees a soul devoid of all healthful soundness but full, instead, of the scars from perjuries and injustice which each of the person's deeds has imprinted on his soul. Such souls, distorted by lies and arrogant pretensions, are wholly devoid of uprightness, being nurtured, as they were, apart from truth. . . . Now I am persuaded by these words, Callicles, and I study how I shall present before the judge there as healthy a soul as possible. Therefore, saying farewell to the honors sought by the many and practicing the truth, I shall really try to live being the best man I possibly can, and when I die to die being the same kind of person.

Such is the Platonic Socrates' statement of his belief—he doesn't claim to *know*—that each person's every voluntary act and deed always leaves some trace of itself within man's deepest inner self. Note that Socrates—or Plato, no one can say which—declares that *each deed* leaves its imprint in one's deepest inner self.

Now if Socrates believed that even evil returned for evil is still evil; if he further believed that all voluntary deeds and attitudes leave some trace of themselves, however slight, within the doer's deepest self and character; if he was also anxious to keep his inner self (his "soul") as free as possible of every blemish of evil; and, finally, if he thought that wronging a person leaves a greater and more certain trace of evil in one's "soul" than being wronged does, then his insistence that, if a choice became necessary, he would always choose to be wronged rather than to wrong another person, becomes quite logical, natural, and reasonable.

Such an interpretation helped to clarify for me an ex parte quotation from St. Paul (Gal. 6:7) which I had often heard: "Don't be deceived; God is not outwitted; for whatsoever a man sows, that he also reaps." This was a puzzling statement to me, and Paul's addition to it was too general to be of much help. I knew of too many men who had sown good will only to reap ill will during their lifetimes, who had sown friendliness, kindness, and justice only to reap injustice, unkindness, and hostility for Paul's statement to mean what it seemed on its face to mean. But in the light of Socrates' statement, Paul perhaps meant "Whatever a man voluntarily sows in attitudes and conduct, that he reaps—not from his fellow man, but in his inner life and character." If that is what Paul meant, his statement becomes quite clear and seems patently true.

Here again the Greeks helped to give me a more meaningful understanding of a most important natural law that seems to have been written into the nature of things, a law that apparently made it possible for man, in his Creator-given freedom, to develop and bring to maturity his highest and most humane possibilities or his worst potentialities, if he, in his freedom, so chooses.

With this idea, the Platonic Socrates again brought into greater clarity for me something I had dimly suspected for quite a while: that the Creator had left at least enough freedom to each person for him to be the ultimate arbiter of what type of person he would choose to become. Incidentally, this faith came practically full circle for me when I read Edwin Markham's statement of it in the final stanza of his "Man-Test":[1]

> I will leave man to make the fatal guess,
> Will leave him torn between the No and Yes;
> Leave him unresting till he rests in Me,
> Drawn upward by the choice that makes him free;
> Leave him in tragic loneliness to choose
> With all in life to win or all to lose.

III   *The Importance of Thinking Rightly*

A third surprising idea to me, one stated rather clearly by the Greeks, is the correlation they saw between right thinking and correct action and outlook. "Not to think wrongly" (*i.e.*, to think rightly) about anything enhanced, as they seem to have believed, the chances of an escape from wrong action and evil consequences, whereas "not to think rightly" (*i.e.*, to think wrongly) assured a distorted relationship that, in turn, made right action impossible and evil consequences all but certain.

The paramount importance of "not thinking wrongly" and also of "not thinking rightly" became clearer and clearer to me as I tried to ferret out what the Greeks appear to have meant by two of their statements on this subject.

The first is in line 927 of Aeschylus' *Agamemnon*: "And not to think wrongly is the greatest gift of god." Agamemnon is pleading with his wife not to honor him as a god or as some barbarian potentate by insisting that he descend from his chariot and make his way into the palace over the rich carpet she had spread for him. He insists—not too convincingly—that such honors should be reserved for the gods (for the gods were quite jealous, as the Greeks thought, of their status and honors, and man arrogated such honors to himself only at the direst peril). Agamemnon is thus afraid some god might behold his act of arrogance and avenge it with dreadful punishment, and he therefore urges his wife not to think wrongly in this matter.

A more complete statement concerning the necessity of thinking rightly in all matters appears near the end of Plato's *Phaedo* (115e). This, Socrates' final dialogue, took place during the morning of the day he was to drink the hemlock. In it, he offers his apologia for the immortality of the soul, and, upon the completion of the discussion, he gave his final instructions to his followers. No sooner had he done this than Crito, an apparent favorite among Socrates' associates, asked the master how they should bury him. Socrates replied: "Any way you wish, if you can catch me."

Socrates then turned and said to the others:

> Won't some of you persuade Crito—all my talk
> has not persuaded him—that, when he sees my
> body being carried out for burial or cremation, he
> is not to think it is I—the real Socrates—who
> is being buried or cremated. Otherwise, he will be
> grieved for me on the ground that I, the real Socrates,
> will be suffering something terrible by being buried
> or cremated. So help him to see that I, the real
> Socrates, who is now speaking with you and conducting the dialogue, will already be gone to some
> blessedness of the blest when my body is being
> buried or cremated.

Then, turning to Crito, Socrates uttered these remarkably wise words:

> For know you well, dear Crito, that not to think
> rightly about a thing not only puts one into

a false relationship with the thing itself, but it also works some evil in one's soul.

There is a kindred but not an exact parallel passage in Plato's *Apology of Socrates* (sec. 28b).

Now just what did the Greeks mean by "not to think wrongly" (*i.e.*, to think rightly) and "not to think rightly" (*i.e.*, to think wrongly)? What they seem to have had in mind had nothing to do with thinking evil thoughts, as one commentator has ventured. These expressions have no moral connotations in the sense that we use the term *moral*.

By "not to think wrongly" and also "not to think rightly" the Greeks apparently meant not to think of anything in any other way than it by nature *really is*. In mathematical terms, they doubtless meant something like this: Not to get the equation wrong is the greatest gift of the gods; otherwise, one cannot get the right answer. In short, the Greeks meant in these passages that man must think rightly about the gods, about himself, and about everything else just as each thing happens by nature to be. Man must think about the laws of life and living just as they happen by nature to be. He must remember his limitations—that he is mortal and must never arrogate to himself rights and privileges that belong to the immortals. The Greeks apparently summed all this up in their famous commandment, "Know thyself": Know your limitations, your abilities and place, and remember that you are mortal and act accordingly.

The Greeks thought that for a mortal to utter blasphemous statements or assume prerogatives belonging to the immortals was an unforgivable arrogance, which they called *hubris* (spelled also *hybris*). Any mortal who allowed himself to become a victim of *hybris* automatically came under the power of Ate, the goddess of infatuation and ruin. At Ate's direction, the victim's sense of values would become so confused that what he might think would save him would actually destroy him, and what he would think would destroy him would actually save him. The goddess would thus lure the victim of *hybris* into his destruction by his own infatuation.

Agamemnon knew, or at least feared, that to enter his palace walking on a carpet richly wrought in purple was too high an honor for mortals. He accordingly urged his wife Clytemnestra not to think wrongly about him; to honor him as a man but not as some superhuman being. He did not persuade her, however. He then, in his pride, permitted himself to enter the palace walking on the daedal carpet, only to be treacherously murdered a bit later by his wife.

Now what about Socrates' admonition to Crito, "Not to think rightly about things not only puts one into a false relationship with them but also works some evil in one's soul"? To understand best what prompted Socrates' remark requires an understanding of the context in which it was made and the conception of death held by the more mature Greeks.

Recall the circumstances: Socrates had just completed with his followers an extended discussion of the soul and its immortality. The dialogue ended with everyone apparently agreeing with the conclusions reached, and Socrates had a right to suppose that all had been convinced. But when Crito asked, "How shall we bury you?"—not just your body but *you*—Socrates knew that at least the real heart of the dialogue had been lost on Crito. There was no time to go into the matter again with Crito, so Socrates urged the others to try to persuade Crito. Then, turning to Crito, he reminded the younger man of how important it is to think rightly about things, particularly about death.

The Greeks, more consistently than any people before them, seem to have regarded living man as a dual creature composed of two rigidly interdependent entities, which they called the body and the soul. They regarded the body as mortal but the soul as immortal. For them, then, death was in reality merely the separation of man's mortal body from the real part of himself. The body, as they saw it, died and returned to the dust, while the soul continued its existence in Hades—among the blessed there, if the judges in Hades found that the soul before them had been just and righteous on earth, or among the tortured if it was adjudged to have been evil and wicked in life. A late anonymous epigram in the *Greek Anthology* expresses well the earlier idea of death among the maturer Greeks:

The body is the soul's constant distress—
Its death, encumbering weight, constraining lot.
But when the soul fares from the body forth,
As being freed from bonds of death,
It flees to god, immortal.

There are occasional references in Pindar, Aeschylus, and Plato to what is thought to be an earlier, more primitive belief that the soul or spirit sometimes left the body during sleep. It would conveniently return to the body before the individual awakened, unless he was suddenly or prematurely aroused from sleep. *Eumenides,* lines 104–5, seems to indicate that dreams were once thought to be the experiences and activities of the soul or spirit while it was freed, through sleep, from the restraints put on it by the body during waking hours.

This does not mean that the Greeks were the first to advance the notion of a soul and body for man, separate but rigidly interdependent in this life. It does mean that as early as the *Odyssey* (about 700 B.C.), the Greek conception was more refined and a bit more definite than earlier ideas of a continuing life for man. (A reproduction of an early sepulchral panel from the eastern Mediterranean region depicts servants and cattle being slain and buried with a nobleman so that they might serve him in his new life. This appears to indicate that the nobleman's new life was believed to be much like life in this world. There was little, if anything, suggested about where this new life was to be lived.)

But by the time of Homer, the Greeks had arrived at a concept of a soul for man that, while being interdependent with the body during this life, could fully separate itself from the body and continue to live on in a lower world known as the "house of Hades," the abode of the underworld's lord. It was divided into regions—Elysium for the reward of the "just and righteous" and other compartments for the punishment and purification of those in need of such. But even Elysium held little, if any, attraction for the Greeks. When Odysseus complimented Achilles on his status even in Hades, Achilles unhesitatingly replied: "I would rather be on earth as a hired laborer for a landless man who had slight means than be king over all these mere wraiths of men who have died." I can recall only one Greek of the classical period—Socrates of Athens—who is portrayed as thinking of his journey into Hades as entering into a happier life. Only with the advent of Christianity, after the locale of future happiness in the afterlife had been transferred from Hades, below the earth, to the heavens above, did death for the righteous come to be regarded as a release from the bondages of this world into a life of freedom, joy, and happiness. Hades (Christian Hell) was left below the earth and reserved for punishment of the wicked.

For Socrates, however, those who regarded death as something dreadful were not thinking rightly. He told the jurymen who had condemned him that death was only a migration of the soul from this region to a realm where demigods and heroes who had lived justly were continuing their existence. And what greater blessedness could there be, he asked the jurymen, than to associate and compare experiences with these, and to see who of them was really just and who merely thought he was?

Readers may wonder why I lay so much emphasis on this Greek idea of the necessity of thinking and therefore feeling rightly about people and things. The chief reason is that I have come to believe, both from observation and experience, that *a man's conduct and attitudes toward anything inevitably gravitate to the level of his thinking and feeling about it.*

Think it out for yourself. Doesn't the shameful and unjust conduct and attitude of so many whites toward blacks stem largely from thinking and feeling wrongly about them in the Greek sense? The myths of congenital inferiority or superiority exemplify such thinking and lead individuals to treat their fellows accordingly. The legions of Hitler regarded the Russians, we are told, as subhuman and treated their Russian captives accordingly.

In a more personal sense, think how many unproductive human relationships are just that because persons think and feel wrongly, first about themselves and then about their neighbors! So much in human experience shows that whoever would expect to enjoy a constructive rapport with anything must first think and feel rightly about it—whether it is an idea, a cause, or another human being.

The necessity to think and feel rightly about matters is accentuated by the present impatient temper of people throughout the world—and of Americans in particular. The human majority seems so impatient for action and excitement that it rushes into decisions and commitments with little reflection on the consequences. Patience for the longer, well-thought-out view of things is lacking except, perhaps, where financial profit and loss are concerned. These kinetic people seem not to understand that thinking and feeling rightly about things are necessary prerequisites for right action and conduct regarding them.

Examples of this haste and impatience for action can be clearly seen in the records of most present legislative bodies. How many hastily conceived legislative transactions, preceded by inadequate thinking and demonstrating no concern as to whether or not the matters being decided and passed have been rightly conceived, have caused society untold mischief—and are still doing so!

Had we Southerners thought and felt rightly about the 1954 school decision of the Supreme Court—our bedrock of law and order—we would never have attempted through legislative subterfuge to resist the mandate so stubbornly. Or note the number of communities, nationwide, that resort to quick, stopgap remedies to meet the educational needs of their children rather than tax themselves enough to give their children the educational advantages they deserve! The Greek thinkers would say that such shortsightedness shows quite clearly that such communities think wrongly about their children, about education, and about money.

In short, Americans appear to have little interest in thinking things through until they feel as confident as possible that they are thinking rightly about them. We insist time and again on the quick and cheaper actions—actions that will tide us over some crisis, but that offer no true solution in perspective. This urge seems especially true among politicians and public servants.

One of the subtlest avenues by which men are lured into thinking wrongly about things is the failure to recognize or remember that, except where concrete material matters are concerned, "words, like nature, only half reveal and half conceal" exact meanings. This is especially true of documents dealing with what have been called spiritual and moral truths and also of those dealing with general legal, economic, social, psychological, and governmental matters. Dealing as they do with intangible and general rather than with specific matters, such statements mean different things to different people at different times, in different places and periods, and under different circumstances. As a result, they must always be properly interpreted before they can be intelligently, correctly, and rightly thought of and applied. Uninterpreted or wrongly interpreted, such statements cannot be used or thought of rightly.

There are at least two ways of ensuring wrong thinking about such generalized documents: One is to suppose, as most people subconsciously do, that a literal interpretation is not an interpretation, even though it is as truly an interpretation as any other is. As a matter of fact, nothing can enter the human mind in any meaningful form until it has been interpreted. The second way to ensure wrong thinking about general statements is to assert or imply that one's particular interpretation is the one and only meaning that the particular statement can have.

One other element in today's milieu that demands considered right thinking more than ever before is the magnitude and increased complexity of practically all the more important phases of our daily life and living. The mere patience and effort involved in thinking sufficiently and rightly about almost anything today is quite forbidding, yet imperative. It is discouraging to hear those in positions of importance announcing almost daily some superficial conclusion they have reached and accepted concerning matters of the highest import and complexity.

We hear educators equating mere training with basic education. We hear politicians proclaiming the indissoluble union—not mere confederation—of their state with that superior entity known as the United States of America and in the next breath proclaiming as inviolable a state sovereignty superior to the sovereignty of the United States. They talk as though it were possible for an individual or a state to enter into a bona fide, indissoluble union with another person or entity and still retain unimpaired their former inviolable sovereignty. Such "reasoning" is a classic example of thinking wrongly—one that puts the cart squarely in front of the horse.

For the citizens of any of the fifty states are (and must be) citizens of the United States *before* they are citizens of any particular state. Therefore, their first allegiance and responsibility are to the United States and its demands, just as truly as the first responsibility and allegiance of any truly married couple are to the sovereignty of the plighted troth that made them one rather than to any sovereignty of their premarital social rights— if they are to remain truly united as one. Whoever thinks rightly in this matter will remember that no citizen's state or home can be any safer than the United States, to which his state is inexorably bound, is safe.

A final example of thinking wrongly can be discerned in what emanates across the land from impatient reformers. They daily announce their intention to force every citizen to come to terms with his conscience, as though every person opposing them had not already come to the terms he finds compatible with his conscience. These reformers apparently assume there is such a thing in adults as an unsullied and unconditioned conscience to which all men should be forced to conform and that they possess it in pure form. But there is no such thing; for reformers to imply that there is seems to be a not very subtle way of saying: "We mean to force citizens to submit to what is congenial to *our* conscience" —which, incidentally, has been modified and conditioned to their own desires and purposes.

These, then, are some rather basic aspects of life and living in regard to which this Greek emphasis on thinking and feeling rightly about things has been of immense help and importance to me. It has enabled me to see and understand many things with a clarity I would never otherwise have experienced.

IV Fruitful Discussion Depends on Compatible Assumptions

The dramatic date for the dialogue recounted in Plato's *Crito* is the day before Socrates was to drink the hemlock, in 399 B.C. That the verdict against Socrates was unjust was known to all; but, since it was properly rendered by a legitimately authorized court, Socrates argued that it was his duty as a law-abiding citizen to abide by it, unless the court would reconsider—which it would not.

His followers, however, wanted to spirit him out of Athens, to live in some other state. But Socrates would not consent to go, unless it could be proved to him that it would be just and right for him to go. To persuade him, they would have to prove to him first of all that *it would be just and right for him to wrong the city of Athens in return* for the wrong it had done him. Convinced as he was that retaliation is always wrong, Socrates wanted to be sure that his departure from Athens, against the city's will, would not be wronging the very one whom least of all he should wrong—his own city, which had enabled him to live a civilized life.

The dialogue makes clear Socrates' perception that, if he and Crito are to discuss this problem in any fruitful and convincing way, he must be sure that Crito also accepts the primary assumption that retaliation for any injustice is always wrong.

26

Socrates then persuades Crito, in about a page of dialogue, that, for the individual committing it, any act of injustice is always an evil and shameful thing in any and all circumstances. If that is true, it can never be right to do wrong; since this is true, one must never return evil for evil, no matter to what extent he has been wronged. When Crito seems ready to agree, Socrates warns him as follows:

> In agreeing to all this, Crito, be sure that you do not do so contrary to your real opinion. For I am quite aware that few are the people to whom these conclusions ever have or ever will seem true. Moreover, between those to whom these conclusions seem true and those to whom they do not, there can be no common grounds for fruitful discussion but they must necessarily scoff at each other as they contemplate each other's arguments.

Understanding this passage has been most helpful to me. It provided a rational basis for the biblical injunction against retaliation (since wrong is always wrong, it can never be right to return wrong for wrong), and it explained why so many debates that begin as reasoned discussions so frequently degenerate into acrimonious contentiousness. The more I thought about Socrates' postulates the more reasonable they seemed. For how can a consciously committed *wrong* be right? And how can discussants, proceeding from contrary or incompatible assumptions, ever reach compatible conclusions, as long as they insist on starting from different or conflicting assumptions?

Observe our attempts to reach acceptable conclusions concerning the priority of property rights versus human rights. One group proceeds from the assumption that property rights rightly take precedence over human rights, while the other assumes that human rights should always be given priority over property rights. Endless—and meaningless—discussion can be the only result. Or how can discussants be expected to reach any equitable agreement on how two different races should be treated when one of them assumes the two races are congenitally equal, while the other insists that one of them is subhuman or certainly inherently inferior? Nor can any common agreement be reached where a citizen's federal and state's rights are in question, as long as one party assumes that the citizen's federal rights are primary, while the other maintains that his state's rights should take precedence. All of which is to say that rational and fruitful conclusions can be reached only from similar or at least compatible assumptions— not from contradictory or incompatible ones.

When discussion sets out from incongruous assumptions, notice how quickly and regularly it degenerates, as Socrates remarked, into what amounts to acrimonious scoffing. The discussants begin politely enough, but soon settle into the litany of false discourse: "That's impossible"; then, "You surely can't believe that," "That's foolish"; then, "That's stupid," "Only a fool could believe that." When I observe this kind of impasse, I feel like exclaiming, "Change to congenial assumptions, or end your 'discussion'; all you are doing now is multiplying and intensifying your differences." I have often wondered if many of the apparent differences and misunderstandings that rend our society today may not be the inevitable results of our trying to wrest compatible and acceptable conclusions from incompatible assumptions—an impossible task for individuals or peoples.

I am not for a moment suggesting that there should be any lessening of discussion, but only that the first order of business in any discussion is to make quite clear the basic assumptions from which each discussant plans to proceed. This must be done if the subsequent discussion is to be an intelligent and convincing one; whatever discussion is necessary to reach this starting point is quite in order.

V Keeping a Clear Line Between Mere Belief and Reasonably Verified Knowledge

Look, if you will, at another idea, also from Socrates: In all of his thinking and statements concerning transcendent or abstract subjects, as opposed to concrete matters, the individual should keep as clearly defined a line as possible between what can be reasonably known and what is and must be only what one thinks or believes. *For no amount of unverifiable belief can constitute verified knowledge.*

One of the greatest intellectual sins I know—and I am sure Socrates would agree—is to present as reasonably verified knowledge what is, in fact, only personal belief or interpretation, even though this may be based on the fullest knowledge then available. If only our public figures, writers, and especially our teachers would keep clear in all they say this distinction between what can be reasonably verified and what still remains, in the present state of knowledge, basically only belief or an educated guess, how much misunderstanding and disillusionment could be avoided.

Socrates employed two methods in keeping clear the critical distinction between what he thought he could reasonably verify and what was only a belief with him. One was the use of such qualifying phrases as "according to what is said" about the matter being discussed or "if the things said about it are true." The other was in his use of myths that his interlocutor might regard as just "myths" or as "old wives' tales," while he *felt* they represented what was true.

An excellent example of Socrates' use of myths to portray something he really believes but cannot verify can be seen near the close of Plato's *Gorgias* (sec. 523 ff.), a dialogue concerned with the just and unjust uses of rhetoric. The final section is a discussion between Socrates and Callicles, a materialistic politician who finds it impossible to accept Socrates' arguments. Though Callicles finally gives up, he decides to go along, giving Socrates the answers he needs to complete his arguments.

Even though Socrates had completed what seemed to him the proper answer to the problem under discussion, he was aware that his answer could not be "proved" by syllogistic reasoning. So, true to his practice of keeping as clear a line as possible between what he could reasonably know and what was in reality personal belief, Socrates resorted to a myth—a kind of parable— to illustrate what he *believed* concerning the matter but could not logically prove to be true. In general terms, the myth was as follows:

In an early age of the world, men were judged on the last day of their lives, by living judges, as to how they should properly fare in the afterlife. This method of judging proved too subjective in values to be just, and Zeus decreed that henceforward men were to be judged in the next world, after death, by judges who had died also. Under this plan, only the souls of men, stripped of their bodies and all meretricious addenda, appeared before the judges in Hades and were judged only on the basis of the condition clearly manifested in the soul itself.

Since every man's soul carried with it into the next world definite marks or scars from his each and every unjust act and from his perjuries and misdeeds, the judges would then have to judge men's souls *only* on the basis of the condition in which the souls came to them. They would therefore judge them more justly and would assign to each soul a more just and fitting punishment.

Socrates then reminds Callicles that he believes (though he does not *know*) that this myth very likely represents what is destined for each individual at his life's end. To such an extent does Socrates believe this to be man's destiny that he has tried all his life to keep his soul as free as possible from scars of evil and injustice so that he might present to the judges in Hades a soul as scar-free as possible. Socrates urges the recalcitrant Callicles to make such an effort himself so that he, too, might keep his soul as unscarred as possible and thus be able to do more than simply gape and appear confused before the questions asked him by the judges in Hades.

A classic example of Socrates' repeated use of such phrases as "if the things said regarding this are true" is found near the end of Plato's *Apology of Socrates* (sec. 40-c4). Socrates is discussing his views of death and the afterlife—ideas in which he genuinely believed but could not prove. Although this passage is less than two pages long in the Greek text, these admonishing phrases are used four times, apparently because Socrates wanted the jurymen to know that he regarded the discussion as an open one. It is true that Socrates regarded some questions as closed, which we no longer consider closed. His consistent insistence that no man willingly does anything he thinks is wrong is an example. But he seems to have gone to considerable lengths to portray as open whatever seemed to him to be open. And I have long been grateful to him for making plain the great importance of defining as clearly as possible in my pronouncements the elements I regard as reasonably known and those that are really only my beliefs or interpretations.

The Greeks used a fullness of expression that is also helpful in dealing with our common tendency to try to pass off as a complete statement or truth what is only an ex parte truth. Even though such statements are fatal to accurate understanding, we hear them offered quite regularly wherever controversial subjects are involved.

Political sloganeering is characterized by such incomplete and therefore misleading statements. "Stand up for America," as used by one party, really means "Stand up for America *as we want it to be*"—which is something quite different. It is a societal cliché of white segregationists to boast of their great "care and concern for blacks," without adding (as their conduct clearly indicates) "so long as blacks stay in their place"—unilaterally assigned to them by the white man.

This tactic of incomplete statement is often apparent in those bits and pieces of quotations that we use in public and private for our special purposes. One of the most flagrant examples I know is one you remember seeing chiseled in simple splendor on buildings on all too many campuses: "You shall know the truth and the truth shall make you free." Both the Greek and the context, of course, make it about as clear as it could be that this New Testament statement is the second conclusion of a very vivid *condition*. In translation: "If you shall abide in this word (*i.e.*, teaching) of mine, you are truly my disciples and you shall know the truth and the truth shall free you" (*i.e.*, make you free). Obviously, the simplistic part generally quoted is thus manifestly not true, except for those who first meet the condition. The statement is valid only after the preceding condition has been met.

The fullness of expression and the concern for exactness of expression that I found so common to the great Greek thinkers made me aware early of the perils in articulating my own thoughts before I defined for myself what it was in them that I *knew* and what it was I *believed*.

VI The Ideal for Democratic Living

In his *Eumenides*, lines 696–7, Aeschylus in 458 B.C. clearly and succinctly stated an idea I have found helpful in trying to evolve a civic outlook fully adequate for democratic living.

Look first at the background for the statement. Over the centuries the Athenians had developed a highly revered court known as the Court of the Areopagus. Aristocratic in composition and outlook, and therefore conservative, this court was rather unsympathetic to liberal Athenian democracy as it developed during the sixth and fifth centuries B.C. As democracy grew in power and influence, the power and influence of this court were more and more curtailed. In the vernacular of our day, this was an early "confrontation" between liberals and conservatives.

The Court of the Areopagus was so old that the history of its origin was not known. Apparently as a gesture of sympathy and approval of the court, Aeschylus turned to his dramatic purpose a legendary account of its origin in his *Eumenides*, lines 481 ff.

He portrays Athene as establishing on the hill of Ares (Areopagus) near the Acropolis a court of twelve judges, under her personal chairmanship. This court was to administer the affairs of the city and adjudicate differences between citizens, especially cases involving homicide. Aeschylus then has Athene lay on the people and the twelve members of the court a sort of general charge, establishing the court as a protection to the city for all time and commanding the citizens to properly fear and revere it always, keeping it pure and unsullied by sordid gain.

In her charge, however, Athene states also the rule by which the citizens of Athens themselves are to live and by which they are to be governed. Translated rather literally, Aeschylus' Athene says: "I advise the protectors [the judges] of the city to sanction neither lawlessness nor any despotism." More clearly and concisely, the sum and substance of her mandate is paraphrased by Mr. E. D. A. Morshead in these words:[2]

> Let no man live uncurbed by law
> Nor curbed by tyranny.

The more I have reflected on that statement and what Aeschylus plainly meant by it, the more it has seemed to me about the best standard and ideal any citizen in a democracy could set for himself. For myself at least, ever since I faced up to the requirements of that statement, I have never lacked for a satisfying criterion by which to measure my civic responsibility to the laws and government of the country in which I live.

One should remember, however, that Athene's mandate is in a late fictional account of the origin of the ancient Court of the Areopagus. The final reforms that cleared the way for the fully realized Greek democracy had been achieved only fifty years earlier, in 508 B.C. Also, the last of the Athenian tyrants had been disposed of only six years before that date. There is little doubt that this young, exuberant democracy needed as much good and binding advice as possible, and I suspect it was no accident that Aeschylus put this mandate in the mouth of Athene, the favorite and most honored goddess of the Athenians.

But, even so, the Athenians gave as little heed to Athene's command as later peoples have. This is not strange, if one considers the adequacy and inclusiveness of her statement. There is a human tendency to reject—sometimes without even attempting—anything approaching the too perfect or ideal. As for myself, I have never found any good reason to abandon a perfect ideal even when I knew I could never satisfy it. It seems to me almost a natural law that a man will never achieve his fullest possibilities as a human being if he undertakes to develop them under the beckoning of any ultimate standard less than perfection.

Even though this wise and true civic ideal has always been well beyond my full grasp, it has never let me down, not even in trying and nihilistic times. It has, rather, sustained me even in such circumstances.

In this mandate, Athene further charges her citizens as follows:

> On this hill [where the Court of the Areopagus was to sit] the reverence of the townsmen and its kinsman, fear, shall restrain the citizens from wrong-doing night and day, so long as the citizens make no innovations in the laws.

This surprised me. Was there a genuine kinship between reverence and fear? Later reflection indicated there were two opposite kinds of fear: one, the fear of what someone or something might do to the person fearing, and the other, the "fear" of what some conduct or attitude of his might do to someone or something deeply cherished and respected by him.

This new concept of reverence as a kinsman of fear was welcome news to one reared, as I was, in a religious climate that made crass fear the chief reason for coming to terms with one's Creator. People in this milieu were told, of course, that the Lord was to be loved; but the prime reason for doing so turned out to be chiefly fear of what He would do to them if they didn't.

This new insight into the nature of reverence cleared up radically for me the biblical declaration that "Fear of the Lord is the beginning of wisdom"—a statement I found repugnant even as it was drummed into me. I felt that the Deity was to be loved rather than feared. But through reflection on Athene's declaration I perceived that reverence, as its etymology showed, was really a differently oriented "fear," having nothing to do with punishment, since it was born of a profound concern not to disappoint or offend someone or something greatly loved and honored.

In the light of this new understanding, my resentment toward the biblical aphorism vanished. I could now honestly believe that, while fear of the Lord might well be the beginning of wisdom, it was only after this fear had matured into a "fear" that amounted to reverence for Him that it could claim the full status of wisdom. Such an interpretation made sense of the biblical passage for me; for this insight I continue to be grateful.

This new concept of a "fear" unconcerned with punishment clarified for me also a basic element in that deferential consideration for parents and loved ones that causes many mature persons to speak and act one way when near their families and quite otherwise when away from them. Their concern is not primarily for themselves but for their loved ones, lest they cause them grief and distress. Such conduct on the part of persons already grown is doubtless rooted in the fact that their childhood fear of punishment has been transmuted as they matured into a deferential love and a respect that keep them ever fearful of offending or hurting those they love and care for deeply.

VII Sense of Right and Wrong Can Be Hopelessly Perverted

As I have tried to comprehend certain things pertinent to the understanding of the true self and the world, an idea found first in Greek literature of the sixth century B.C. has seemed to me of great value. The earliest full statement of this idea is found in the "Proverbs" of Theognis of Megara, who is said to have lived in the latter part of that century.

Stated in modern terms, Theognis' thought is this: Man can abuse, distort, and debilitate his innate sense of generally recognized right and wrong until the sense becomes completely demoralized and will no longer function in trustworthy fashion. This belief of the Greeks held, further, that the critical moral sense can, in fact, degenerate and become so perverted that the individual will inevitably come to regard the good as evil and the evil as good. The perversion of values can continue until it becomes irreversible, leaving the victim wholly unable thereafter to distinguish rightly between what is right and what is wrong. From that point, his destruction is certain. He will regard the good that would save him as evil destined to ruin him, and the evil that would ruin him as good ready to aid him.

After warning his friend not to be overeager about anything, Theognis specifically advises that

> Often a man, eager for distinction in his pursuit of gain, is readily misled by some favoring deity into greater and greater wrong-doing until he easily comes to think that what is really evil is good and what is actually good is evil. (lines 402–6.)

A chorus in Sophocles' *Antigone* expresses the same perception:

> Someone wisely uttered this famous saying: to the man whose mind some god is luring into ruinous delusion, sooner or later evil comes to seem to that man good; and for the briefest time he lives apart from evil. (*Antig.* 620–25.)

Notice that Sophocles omits the last part of Theognis' statement "and good is evil." This omission *may* mean that by Sophocles' time the full idea was so well known that the latter half would be understood any time the first half was mentioned. An early Greek commentator adds what he apparently considers a clarifying sentence: "Whenever a deity is preparing evil for a man, he first of all perverts the mind with which the man makes his plans."

A variant of the idea, which the Greek orator Lycurgus attributes to some of the ancient poets, is mentioned by him in the 92nd section of his speech (330 B.C.) *Against Leocrates*:

> When an angry deity decides to work evil on a person, he first of all takes fully from the man sound understanding and plants within him a worse judgment that he may not discern his errors.

41

Clearly, the Greeks seem to have concluded from their experience and observation that man's inner self and powers could be as irrevocably ruined through specious rationalizations, wrong use, or nonuse as any physical organ or power can be.

That the Greeks attributed this ruination of man's ability to distinguish good from evil to a god should not surprise anyone or compromise the worth of the basic idea. God leading man into temptation has been a frequently expressed concept from early times. The Old Testament has many examples, and one of the petitions in the Lord's Prayer is "and lead us not into temptation." (Commentators have tried to convert that petition into something more congenial to modern thinking, but without much success.)

Few modern theologians still subscribe to the belief that God leads man into temptation for the purpose of harming him. Some argue that man may be led into temptation, as Jesus of Nazareth is said to have been, for the purpose of testing man, of clarifying his uncertainties, and thus strengthening the man. But we still have no ultimate, convincing explanation of why some persons seem consciously to drive themselves into ruin. What is now spoken of as compulsive conduct—a descriptive term, incidentally, and not an explanation—was attributed by the Greeks to a god.

Shakespeare's excellent summation of this Greek idea presumes that the man himself—not a god—is responsible for the destruction of his ability to distinguish good (even for himself) from evil. The only role given the Deity by Shakespeare is that of ensuring resulting confusion and ruin for the violator. His *Antony and Cleopatra* (Act III, scene xiii, lines 136–40) declares:[3]

> But when we in our viciousness grow hard,
> (O misery on it), the wise gods seal our eyes
> In our own filth, drop our clear judgments, make us
> Adore our errors, laugh at us while we strut
> To our confusion.

A modern statement of this Greek feeling would leave the Deity out entirely as a direct agent. It would hold man's voluntary or deterministic choices and conduct —plus the natural and inevitable consequences—responsible for the human predicament.

Better than any explanation I have so far encountered, this theory of man's being able to pervert his native ability to distinguish what is good from what is evil until it actually functions oppositely from what it should, explains more naturally and reasonably for me the monstrous conduct of even highly civilized men. It is not an obvious explanation of such conduct, but one that requires some earnest thought to see how natural and reasonable it is, the result of a sort of insidiously induced moral brainwashing.

No better or more arresting modern example of this fatal human malady exists than that found in the dedicated devotees of the vicious throwback in human development called Nazism. Nazism originated in one of the most highly civilized societies the world has ever known, and was tolerated for more than a decade. Despite its learning and training, segments of the society had

43

allowed their national pride and visceral yearning for revenge to vitiate and distort their innate or learned senses of right and wrong and of good and evil. Finally, the ability to distinguish between them was lost and with it the interest they once had in such distinctions. The ultimate inability—even after defeat—to acknowledge any evil or wrongness in what they advocated and did, accords well with this explanation.

Moreover, it seems clear that many of the policies and practices the Nazis thought would assure their aims actually contributed to defeat. The determination to deflect and delimit valid scientific knowledge to that which would contribute to their purposes, which they interpreted as good, deprived them of scientists and scientific knowledge that could have aided the national military and economic effort.

The sincere nihilist, it seems to me, usually arrives at that point because he has irrevocably corrupted his natural powers of moral discrimination. He has come to believe that what is really good is actually evil and vice versa. He will readily deny that there is any such thing as moral law or genuine norms in the make-up of the universe. I am not referring to mentally diseased or deranged people, but to those whose minds function well enough in implementing their purposes but whose sense of values and interpretative abilities have been so distorted and corrupted that they can no longer interpret anything correctly either for their purposes or in their own true interest.

Tyrants are frequently victims of this self-induced

malady. In Euripides' *Bacchae*, Pentheus, king of Thebes, despite earnest efforts by his grandfather Cadmus, by Teiresias the chief priest of Thebes, and even by the god Dionysus to persuade him to change, continues to misinterpret the actions and motives of the Bacchanals and to show hostility towards those participating in the Bacchic rites. But Pentheus interprets every effort to save him as a subtle plan to bring ruin and corruption into his kingdom. He therefore spurns all the suggestions of those who would save him and thus brings on himself the very destruction against which they had warned him.

Creon, king of Thebes, provides another example. In an arrogant reliance on his royal power, he blasphemously scorned the divine warning and urging of Teiresias, the chief seer of Thebes, who implored Creon to bury the corpse of his nephew Polyneices. Teiresias had learned through auguries that birds were polluting the altars of the gods throughout the city of Thebes with flesh from Polyneices' corpse and that Creon was inviting retribution by his arrogance. Yet Creon contemptuously told Teiresias that Polyneices' corpse would not be buried, even if the eagles of Zeus should pollute his altars in the heavens with Polyneices' flesh. Because he haughtily rejected Teiresias' warnings as well as the well-intentioned pleadings of his son and his niece, Creon brought on himself the destruction of his kingdom and that of his entire family. He had apparently yielded to that unforgivable arrogance, which made him a victim of *hybris*. And, according to Greek feeling,

45

hybris always brought on the victim that confusion and ruin of his sense of values which would bring him to ruin through his own misjudgments.

Incidentally, I wonder if those religious teachers who accused even Jesus of being in league with Beelzebub, the prince of the devils, and of working through and for him, had not declined into this state of a hopelessly perverted sense of right and wrong or good and evil. Jesus clearly implied that their charge against his work and conduct was blasphemous slander against the Holy Spirit (called also the Spirit of Truth)—a sin that was forever unforgivable, both in this world and in the world to come, according to Matthew's account. The context and details of Jesus' reply to their charge against him and his work seem to indicate that Jesus thought they had lost all ability to discern between the works of a good spirit and those of an evil spirit. For they readily branded his good and humane works as works of the Devil.

Isaiah also had apparently witnessed this state of an irrevocably perverted sense of moral values operating in men of his day, some 700 years before the time of Jesus. In Isaiah 5:20 we find this statement, according to the Revised Standard Version: "Woe to those who call evil good and good evil, who put darkness for light and light for darkness, who put bitter for sweet and sweet for bitter." This reads like an elaboration of the corresponding Greek idea.

The idea, clearly stated and emphasized by the Greeks, that an individual can so abuse and even destroy his sense of values and of good and evil that this sense can no longer function in any trustworthy manner, has been a constant warning to me. It seems to me perilous indeed, if not fatal, to the moral and spiritual self and health to tamper, through specious rationalizations or in any other way, with this Creator-given ability to discern between good and evil.

VIII *Unavoidable Suffering Can Prove Creative, If . . .*

The playwright Aeschylus' comments on suffering have long intrigued me, and I constantly find new meanings in them. In lines 176–81 and in 250–1 of the long initial chorus of the *Agamemnon*, Aeschylus describes the law, fixed by Zeus, that man shall learn through suffering, even though he may not wish to:

> For Zeus it was who set man on the path to thought and wisdom [thoughtful understanding], who fixed with full authority the law that man shall learn through suffering. In sleep therefore there creeps before the heart the memory of painful toil, imparting wisdom to those who wish it not. . . . To those who have suffered, Justice weighs out knowledge.

In those lines Aeschylus is reminding the Greeks that unavoidable suffering, that universal human lot, is neither fatal nor futile. At least it does not have to be so, for how uncalculated suffering affects the individual depends on how he reacts to it. Resentment or a refusal to come to terms with suffering will crush and embitter the man. But if one enters into it, resolved to make the most and best possible of it, it is literally true that much of value can be learned from suffering. The individual's reaction is the key.

Remember, however, that the law of constructive

and creative learning through suffering seldom seems to hold for calculated, mere sadistic, or masochistic suffering, or for suffering planned as revenge. It *can* apply to the uncalculated suffering that comes to one through his own or through some other person's folly, or in the mere business of daily living.

There seem to have been in man's history at least five rather distinct theories regarding the role of suffering in human life. The first is simply that suffering is inexplicable. There is nothing man can do about it except endure it the best he can—much as he does the weather—or ignore it, if he can.

But suffering is too persistent and frequently too poignant to be so ignored. Thus, a second conception of suffering gained currency, at least among the more irreverent. This concept apparently grew out of resentment and declares that suffering is a cruel and unjust element in life that no just creator would ever have allowed. The only possible courses, then, are two: endure it stoically, or continually berate it and the Creator who would permit such a blot on His creation.

This simplistic "explanation" could not long be satisfactory, even to those who espoused it. Consequently, a third explanation of the role of suffering soon found its way into men's thinking. This is called *the punitive conception of suffering,* since it held that the role of suffering was to punish all who broke or were indifferent to the laws of life, whether natural laws or those of social living. There are many examples of the punitive conception in the Old Testament. The Israelites will sin against their God; He will involve them in some kind of suffering; they will repent, and their God will take away their suffering.

I sometimes call this the *big stick* theory of suffering. According to it, suffering was created for the specific purpose of forcing men, through the threat of unpleasant consequences, to obey those laws and demands which had been designed for their moral and spiritual health and development. Within the framework of this perception, man was enabled to see also that unsought and unavoidable suffering was neither futile nor meaningless—if properly accepted and entered into rather than resented.

The fourth theory of suffering holds that suffering exists to teach and instruct man, and man on his part exists to learn. This is called technically *the disciplinary theory of suffering.* (*Disciplinary* is used here in its original Latin sense of *designed for learning or training.*) Clearly, this is the role of suffering that Aeschylus says Zeus had definitively fixed for mankind. He says, you remember, that Zeus compels men to learn wisdom through suffering, *whether they wish to or not.*

The second Isaiah (chapters 42–66) apparently concluded that Yahweh used the sufferings of the Hebrews during their forty-eight-year exile in Babylon to teach them that He was not only their God but the God of all nations as well—an idea earlier resisted. The Jews were to be henceforward His suffering servants whom He was giving "as a light to the nations to open the eyes of the blind, and to bring from their prison those who sit in darkness, that his salvation might reach to the ends of the earth" (42:6–7 and 49:6). That the suffering achieved its purpose accords well with the new Hebrew cosmopolitanism so frequently mentioned or implied throughout the second Isaiah.

The ability of suffering to teach, when one rightly accepts it and enters into it, is demonstrable. The mutual agonies of troops in combat have permanently lifted many above racism. The suffering they jointly experienced with those they had previously regarded as inferior to themselves was so overpowering as to negate the previous feeling. The depth of the learning made possible through suffering is also remarkable. Even genuine bereavement (a form of suffering) "can be the deepest initiation into the mysteries of human life, an initiation more searching and profound than even happy love." So says Dean Inge of St. Paul's Cathedral in London.[4] Christianity was born in suffering and has generally been at its best in times and conditions of distress and misery. As we shall see, moreover, in our next and final conception of the role of suffering in the life of man, suffering, when properly accepted and entered into, can lead one into an understanding—not a mere explanation—of some of the deepest and greatest of life's mysteries.

The fifth conception of suffering, as it pertains to man, is so strongly implied in the fourth theory that it is considered a kindred part of it. But whereas the fourth theory is affirmative in the sense that it sees suffering as a means for teaching man, it is nonetheless only that. The final theory is quite different. It concerns itself with the creative effect the lessons man learns from suffering may have on him.

Technically we refer to this interpretation of the

role of suffering in human life as *the redemptive theory*. The term "redemptive" is unfortunate in this connection, however, since its religious connotations and connections are too strong and extensive to be easily submerged. Actually the term, as it is used here, should carry *no* religious implications or associations. Here it means the bringing of one's humane possibilities and powers of comprehension and understanding to a greater and fuller fruition and maturity through suffering.

The creative power of suffering explains how Oedipus, who suffered more terribly than any figure in Greek tragedy, comes to the end of his life as the noblest, most adequate, most humane, and most understanding character among the great tragic heroes. When Theseus tells Oedipus that Athens needs no aid against Thebes, since the relationship between the two cities is excellent, Oedipus enlightens him. Listen to how deeply and adequately, according to Sophocles, Oedipus had come to understand the eternal rhythm of the nature of things:

> O dearest son of Aegeus, to gods alone comes never
> age nor death;
> But on all else all-mastering time his sure con-
> fusion works.
> Both strength of earth and strength of body wane;
> Faith dies while faithlessness buds forth,
> And never the same spirit of friend to friend or city
> unto city long remains;
> For soon to some and later unto others
> Things pleasant turn to bitter and then again to joy.
> So, if now your affairs with Thebes are all fair-weather,
> Immeasurable time, as it goes on,

52

Brings into being countless days and nights
In which your present profitable pledges
Will for small reason be voided by the spear.

Listen also to Sophocles' description of the passing of Oedipus:

And by what fate it was that Oedipus won his release
   from life,
No living man save Theseus e'er can tell.
No lightning flash accomplished it
Nor any sea-storm wakened at the time;
But some one of the gods conveyed him thence,
Or else the nether depth, in griefless welcome,
Did rend itself for him.
For without moan and pained by no disease
Did Oedipus depart this life, a passing
Truly wondrous, if any mortal ever such has known.

(I have often wondered if such a portrayal of Oedipus' passing was not Sophocles' affirmative comment on the role of suffering in human life. I cannot know, but I wonder.)

Suffering properly accepted and entered into by the sufferer is a frequent theme in later literature of our own English culture. Recall John Milton's "Sonnet on His Blindness."

When I consider how my light is spent
Ere half my days in this dark world and wide,
And that one talent which is death to hide
Lodged with me useless, though my soul more bent
To serve therewith my Maker, and present
My true account, lest He returning chide; . . .

Milton's spirit of active acceptance, though not an easy one, and his resolve show again in the proem to the third book of *Paradise Lost*:

So much the rather thou, celestial Light,
Shine inward and irradiate the mind
Through all her powers; there plant eyes;
All mists from thence purge and disperse
That I may see and tell of things invisible
To mortal sight.

Mr. Churchill could declare in his moving radio address to the British people in the midst of their sufferings on September 11, 1940:[5] "We shall draw from the very heart of suffering itself the means of inspiration and survival"; Paul Geren says in his *Burma Diary*:[6] "Suffering is the supreme experience of community among men. . . . It makes brothers of us."

There are few clearer examples of the insights un-merited suffering, properly accepted, can bring to a person than George Matheson's remarkably beautiful poem "O Love That Will Not Let Me Go." He says it came full-blown out of a deeply traumatic experience of suffering. What this experience was he does not say. The first stanza will show how completely he must have accepted the experience:

O love that will not let me go,
I rest my weary soul in Thee;
I give Thee back the life I owe
That in thine ocean depths its flow
    May richer, fuller be.

54

Through all this discussion, however, it should be clear that if the suffering leaves the sufferer *essentially the same person*—no better, no richer inwardly, no more adequate in attitudes, motives, purposes, or in understanding of the deeper humane possibilities inherent within him—it cannot be regarded as redemptive suffering. For suffering to be redemptive, it must be actively and creatively accepted into an individual's life and thinking in such an absolute way that it becomes an active ingredient within himself, making him a different, a better, and a more adequate person.

Obviously, not everyone is capable of gaining a redemptive experience from suffering. An ability and a readiness to grow in maturity and the possession of healthy psychological needs are requisites. The individual with unusual psychological needs—the sadist or masochist—can seldom profit redemptively from *any* form of suffering. He may accept suffering and live with it stoically, but only in a passive rather than in a creative way. An occasional sufficiently mature and noble-natured individual in, for example, a racial group subjected as a group to calculated suffering may, very occasionally, accept such suffering in such a way as to be redemptively affected by it. But it is a dangerous argument to find value in such an outcome. Certainly there is no case at all for coolly calculated suffering inflicted on a single individual with the intention of affecting him redemptively.

Finally, there is no one and only test to show who has and who has not been redemptively affected by suffering. Only the one so affected knows whether it was suffering or something else that brought him his redemptive outlook on life and its problems. For the redemptive fulfillment of one's fuller humane possibilities can be effected by experiences other than unavoidable suffering. It can be produced in certain sufficiently mature and receptive people by a genuinely uncalculating love. A few years back, one of the better-known actresses told in an article in the magazine section of *The New York Times* of the complete revolution produced in her outlook, thinking, and understanding of some of the deeper mysteries of life, by her realization that her second husband (I think it was) loved her with such a love—a love based on what she was, and on no extraneous matters. Even the roles she had been playing for several seasons suddenly, with the knowledge of this love, became wholly new for her, and she realized how inadequate and unsatisfying her previous performances must have been.

There are also a few choice souls—I think of Anne Frank and Mahatma Gandhi—who seem either to be born redemptively oriented or to become thus oriented so early in life that even unavoidable suffering merely verifies their already attained redemptive humaneness.

It is important to remember that this redemptive experience can happen to the uneducated as readily as it can to the educated. It does not depend on formal sophistication.

These qualifications need to be kept in mind, if the legitimate meaning and proper effects of the redemptive theory of suffering are to be kept in a legitimate perspective. Remember also that it is rather those unmerited and unavoidable sufferings involved in the uncertainties of birth, of growing up, and of the mere business of normal living which, when rightly accepted and made a creative part of one's self, can produce in a properly responsive person a greater adequacy and nobility of character. Unavoidable suffering—as the Greeks knew —does not have to be either futile or fatal.

IX *Evil and Man's Ultimate Mission*

In a digression in the *Theaetetus* (sec. 176), the Platonic Socrates first gave me a rational reason for evil in the world and a new concept of man's ultimate mission in life.

Prior to that encounter I had heard the origin and purpose of evil described in several ways: as an insoluble problem; as an ugly blot on creation, which no just Deity would have allowed; that it had no constructive purpose for man and his problems; that it was created by a totally evil deity, wholly different from the Deity who had created the rest of the world.

And, in the society in which I grew up, man's supreme mission in life was most generally said to encompass a preparation for life after death in some other world, a "service to the Lord," and the "saving of other men's souls." Little was said about man's "working out his own salvation in fear and trembling" as Paul once suggested (Phil. 2:12).

In the light of these early teachings, imagine my surprise when I first encountered the reasonable suggestion of Socrates that it is impossible to do away with evil in this world without neutralizing any realization of the good born *potentially* in every man! It seemed almost heresy, and the further declaration that evil had no place among the gods—who needed no further perfecting—but that its active sphere was in this region here and in our mortal nature opened a whole new concept to my thinking. We must try, therefore, the statement reasoned, to escape, just as far as possible, from the standards, values, and ideals of men into that region of perfect justice. And the suggested means of escape was *through our becoming as like unto God as possible* "in justice and holiness conjoined with wisdom."

Socrates' presentation of this concept occurs in a digression with his interlocutor Theodorus concerning the difference in outlook and practice between a philosopher, reduced to the role of an orator, and a regular public orator. Theodorus finally exclaims:

> If you could persuade everyone of what you say as completely as you have persuaded me, Socrates, there would be more peace and less evil among mankind.

Whereupon, Socrates, centering his thought on Theodorus' implication that evil could be eliminated from our human lot, replies:

> It is not possible to do away with evil, Theodorus— since the good must always have something contrary to itself to oppose it—nor must evil be allowed any place among the gods. Its roaming place is of necessity this region here and in our mortal nature. We must try therefore to flee as quickly as possible [in our thinking] from this region here to that region there [where no evil dwells]. And our means of flight is through our becoming as like unto God as possible— a likeness grounded in justice and holiness conjoined with wisdom. . . .

> For, since God is never unjust to any extent at any time but is always perfectly just, there is nothing more like unto God than whoever of us shall become as just as [is humanly] possible. . . .

To be confronted with the idea that man's innate goodness was only *potential* goodness and that it needed an active adversary wholly contrary to itself for it to be transmuted into active, realized goodness was an intellectual experience for which I was quite unprepared.

But the more I pondered the idea, the nearer it seemed to truth. Many colors have unrealized potential beauty until a different contrary or complementary substance brings out the full tints and hues. I had noticed also that individuals appeared to me to have developed a sounder and more adequate character after enduring a proper amount of adversity than was realized in those who had gone untested in a society of ease and complacency.

Moreover, it seemed illogical, in retrospect, to expect potential goodness to be evolved into full-blown goodness through stimulation from a goodness identical with itself. Such stimulation would merely augment further the *potential state* of man's possible goodness through a kind of inbreeding—which is generally bad—and it would inhibit, so to speak, the developmental powers inherent in man's potential goodness. With all this in mind, I concluded that Socrates' statement regarding the role of evil in human life was doubtless true and more rational than other explanations.

Equally significant to me was the *constructive* means—lacking in other concepts—proposed by Socrates for escaping evil. Granted that his proposal for escape from evil in this world and in ourselves through becoming as like unto God as possible in justice and holiness conjoined with wisdom was a formidable task, it was nonetheless affirmative and creative.

In interpreting his proposal for escape, it will be necessary—if one is to evaluate properly Socrates' feeling in it—to remember how the Greek thinkers had come to feel about justice and about God from the latter part of the fifth century on.

By this time, the Greeks regarded justice not as mere legalistic equity, but as justice based on what was humanely right—on what was demanded by "the firm, unwritten laws of God which live forevermore," to use Sophocles' phrasing. In other words, by the time of Socrates, the Greek conception of moral justice was much like that advocated by the more humane moralists among other peoples and nations. As we read much in the Old Testament about holiness, divine justice, and righteousness, so we read rather much in Socrates' time of a suprahuman justice, of holiness, and of wisdom and truth.

The Greek conception of their supreme god Zeus had also evolved greatly by Socrates' time. It had grown so much that Socrates uses the simple term *god*—meaning a god who is wholly good and free from any kind of evil at any time—far more frequently than he does the term *Zeus*.

Just how much Zeus had grown in godlikeness of character from the Zeus of Homer and the early poets can be surmised from a 38-line *Hymn to Zeus* written

by the Stoic Cleanthes about a century later than Plato's
Theaetetus:

> Most glorious of Immortals, many-named,
> All-powerful forever, nature's ruler,
> Zeus, guiding all through law, all hail!
> For right it is all mortals should invoke thee.
>
> We are thy offspring; we alone, of all
> Mortality that lives and creeps on earth,
> Have been allotted the image of the One.
> Therefore I'll always hymn thee, and always sing thy
>   power.
> Thee all the whirling cosmos meekly follows
> Where'er thou leadest, gladly ruled by thee.
>
> The undying, fiery, two-edged thunderbolt
> Thou holdest in thy hands invincible—
> A minister of power beneath whose stroke
> All nature shudders. With this thou dost direct—
> Great as thou art, supreme king over all—
> The great and lesser lights, and moving ever
> Throughout the universe. No work is wrought
> Apart from thee, O God, not in the sea
> Nor in the heavenly regions nor on earth,
> Except what wicked men do in their folly.
> Thou knowest how to render smooth the rough,
> And how to create order from disorder.
> And things to us unlovely are lovely unto thee.
> So into one has all been framed by thee,
> The evil with the good, that throughout all
> Eternal universal reason reigns.
>
> The wicked by not heeding this fall on
> An evil lot. And some, though ever yearning
> To gain the good, mark not nor ever heed

Thy universal law, which did they heed,
They would obtain and have a goodly life,
One harmonized with reason. But as it is,
Unheedful of the good, they rush about,
One to one thing, another to another;
Some with contentious striving for renown;
And others recklessly intent on gain.
Still others, through impatience for indulgence
And bodily pleasures, win just the opposite.

But thou, who givest all, enthroned in clouds,
Zeus, lord of thunder, deign to save mankind
From grievous ineptitude. Disperse it far,
O Father, from their souls; and grant to them
To obtain that knowledge which enables thee
To govern all with justice, so that we,
Thus honored, may be brought to honor thee,
Hymning thy works always, as all men should;
Since neither for immortals nor for mortals
Is there a greater prize or honor than
Duly to hymn forever the universal law.

What a far cry is this Zeus from the frequently
petulant and philandering Zeus of the early Greek
writers. Note, too, the poet's feeling of reverence and
awe, a feeling that I think is transmitted even to readers
today.

Socrates clearly had in mind some such god when
he declared we must become as like unto god as possible
in justice and holiness conjoined with wisdom. Notice
that Socrates does not suggest that we must try to be
like god in power, glory, or status, but in those moral
and character attributes essential for acting justly and
thus paying our due to man and for paying our due to

god through dedicated holiness and wisdom. The emphasis is on conduct and not on any special position or control over things or others.

Socrates' emphasis here reminds me of the most satisfactory definition of religion I have been able to conceive:[7] *Religion at its best and in its ultimate purpose is God and man extending themselves to each other in the cooperative enterprise of man's becoming more and more like unto God in his attitudes, his motives, and his purposes.*

Man knows, of course, just as Socrates did, that this is a goal he can never reach, but one that is necessary for his fullest self-realization. For he knows also, just as Socrates doubtless did, that he can never hope to realize his fullest divine possibilities for humaneness and character achievement if he takes anything less than perfection as the ultimate standard at which to aim.

Such seems to me a reasonable interpretation of Socrates' words in the *Theaetetus*. One can see that his insight and judgment concerning possible human character attainment were high indeed and rich with hope and promise. Such, at least, is the feeling of one reader who has found this assertion of his both helpful and encouraging.

χ The Role and Function of Love

The ideas of love among the Greeks and among the Athenians especially are among the most difficult in all Greek thought to make clear. Love and just how a people feel about it is difficult to make clear in any culture, but it is doubly difficult to get a fair hearing for the various concepts of love among the fifth- and fourth-century Athenians for three reasons: the fact that the Greeks had four different words for love that, though different in origin—and doubtless in meaning at first—*came very early to be used interchangeably*; the apparent prevalence of homosexuality among the Athenians; and the later arbitrary pre-empting by Christian exegetes and apologists of one of the Greek words for love, compounded by their insistence that it had always signified *only* a very special kind of love. This they called *divine love* as that love came to be portrayed in the New Testament and to be demanded of all Christians.

Let's look first at the four Greek words for love. What was apparently the earliest of these words is *EROS*, which comes from a stem *ER-A-*, meaning to desire, yearn for, desire passionately. Originally the word represented that force which drew together male and female elements throughout the cosmos for the purpose of procreating their kind. Even though it also later came to denote decidedly warm affection and feelings for various things—and even for persons—without any sexual implications, it remained the proper word to use wherever sexual feelings were a factor. (The ode to *Eros* in Euripides' *Hippolytus* (line 525 ff.) shows just how powerful the Greeks thought *Eros* could be.)

The second Greek verb meaning love is *PHI-LÉ-O*, the noun being *PHI-LÍ-A*. These words come from a stem *PHIL-* whose root meaning seems to be unknown. Its meaning must have been quite congenial to Greek feeling, since the Greek dictionary has ten double-columned pages of words compounded with the stem *PHIL-*. *PHI-LÉ-O* meant to the Greeks, "to love, be fond of, have genuine affection for, welcome as a friend." It meant also to kiss, generally as a sign of real affection—not as a mere formal greeting. (The opposite of this verb in meaning was the verb for hate *MI-SÉ-O*, from which English gets the *mis-* in *misanthrope*.) In general terms, *PHI-LÉ-O* was used to express, with or without sexual designs, that general and intimate love and affection characteristic of affectionate families and warm friends.

A third verb for love in Greek is *STÉR-GO*. It means to love, be quite fond of, and is thus much like *PHI-LÉ-O* in meaning. It seems to have been used especially where mutual love was concerned, as among parents and children, or some larger group where a familylike relationship was thought of—the love of a king for his people or a people for its king. It seems to be used very seldom with sexual implications. In some way or other *STÉR-GO* developed also the meaning "to be contented with."

The fourth Greek verb for love was A-GA-PÁ-O, the noun being A-GÁ-PE. Until about the beginning of the twentieth century, the stem of this verb was thought to be akin to the stem of the Greek verb Á-GA-MAI meaning to wonder at, admire, venerate, be pleased or contented with. The newer Greek lexicon, however, doesn't seem so sure of this kinship. But whether these two verbs come from kindred stems or not, one of A-GA-PÁ-O's early meanings was "to be contented or well-pleased with." Just how such a general meaning of this verb got transmuted into "to love, to welcome, greet, or receive with affection"—merely honest affection, without any self-interest or designs of any kind on the person so greeted or welcomed—is not known. Even though the Greeks doubtless felt, as we do, that there is no such thing as a completely selfless love between humans, the verb A-GA-PÁ-O seems to have expressed for the Greeks a concept of love as near as possible to a selfless love. It is no wonder, therefore, that this was the verb used by the early Christian writers to denote their concept of Christian or brotherly love. For the Greeks, however, A-GA-PÁ-O referred to human love, often at its best and purest—"with less of earth in it than heaven"—and not any kind of special divine love, as Christian exegetes have long tried to maintain—a love known only to God and to whomever He, in His wisdom, might impart it.

It is quite important to remember that the love represented by A-GA-PÁ-O was a warm, passionless human love and not some cold, legalistic, other-worldly love; for, as Bridges and Weigle say:[8] "Anything that would tend to separate human love from divine love . . . is wrong." To separate Christian love from any and all human love is preposterous, of course. By such a separation the way is laid wide open for the sadistic and cruel-natured to sublimate their cruelties under the guise of Christian love. Yet to call such rationalized conduct love is as violent a misnomer as I have ever encountered. This divorcing of Christian love from all normal humaneness of human love is doubtless what justified medieval churchmen and civil rulers in torturing "heretics" to make them recant and thus save their souls as well as the Church's doctrines.

Despite the cynicism in vogue today, there are individuals who know from their own experience that there is a human love in which sex, for example, is so secondary as to be regarded as bordering on the irrelevant. But because the kind of human love being discussed here is one not readily induced by the customary calculated means, many will regard it as theoretical but nonexistent love. Nevertheless, those who have experienced such love declare it is real. It appears to grow out of a certain instant appeal and beneficent lift to all that is best in human nature and feelings that some persons experience whenever they come into the presence of the one who so affects them.

If the Greeks knew such love—and I suspect that some few did—I feel sure that they would have used A-GA-PÁ-O as the proper verb for it.

So much for the Greek verbs for love. It is important to remember that, even though these verbs were different in origin (and in meaning, originally), *the ac-*

cumulated evidence shows that they came, in time, to be used frequently interchangeably, especially PHI-LÉ-O and A-GA-PÁ-O. The reason is quite simple: The origins and original meanings of these verbs were forgotten—as happens in all languages—and only their general meaning of love was remembered and therefore used without distinction. One sure way of distorting an author's meaning is to go back and read into his statement the original meaning of the words he uses rather than the meaning demanded by the context. For *it is the context in which a word is used and not its original root meaning that determines the proper meaning to be given that word in a particular context.*

Now the real object of concern in this chapter is the level to which Socrates raises love, *Eros,* in Plato's *Symposium* (201d–212c)—even love between men. But before considering and passing judgment on Socrates' lyrical presentation, one should understand how extensively women, except for an occasional talented courtesan of some important politician, were kept out of public life, social and otherwise, in Athens. This is difficult to understand and hard to believe. But the evidence is overwhelming that the Athenians believed literally in keeping the women at home and telling them little or nothing.

Listen to the following strictures placed on women from about 500 to 338 B.C., the Golden Age of Greece. A woman never enjoyed an individual status, since she was born and kept in the power of her father (or nearest male kin) until she was married, when she was transferred into the power of her husband. She was given little education, on the ground that she was intellectually too inferior for it, and almost all forms of outdoor recreation were closed to her. She was to spend most of her time in the women's separate quarters in the house and be seen and "talked about as little as possible, either for praise or for blame," as Thucydides has Pericles say. The fifth-century Greek girl or woman seldom went out, unless it was to a woman's festival, a procession, a sacrifice, or possibly a dramatic performance that was part of a religious festival. When she did go out, she had to be accompanied by a slave or some other attendant, apparently not her husband or fiancé. There were no customary practices by which a wife could associate socially with her husband's friends. The Athenian husband could divorce his wife almost at will, but the wife could divorce her husband only through the courts and then only on very serious charges. Yet, despite all these strictures, there are epitaphs that seem to testify to a genuine affection held for a husband and a deep sorrow at losing him.

(This Asiatic attitude toward women was not true for all Greece, nor was it the practice in Ionian (i.e., Attic) culture at all periods. Spartan women were so honored and powerful that Sparta was regarded as close to a matriarchy. This more European attitude toward women, which was characteristic of Sparta, was also prevalent in early Greece, as the Homeric poems make clear. Just how or why this European outlook on women came, in the late sixth century B.C., to be supplanted, in Attica especially, by an Asiatic attitude for well over a century has not been convincingly explained as far as I know. In the fourth century B.C., amid a growing cosmo-politanism, the Athenians began to return to the European conception of woman's ability and rightful place in human society—a movement that was hastened by the conquests and cosmopolitanism of Alexander the Great of Macedonia from 336 to 323 B.C.)

The position of the female population of fifth-century Athens was such, then, that isolation from practically all public life, both social and otherwise, resulted. Yet Athens was the most enlightened, open, and liberal city in Greece. A culture so oriented made it all but impossible for Athenian boys and girls as well as young men and maidens to meet and associate with each other. There were no mixed parties, games, or contests of any consequence nor any mixed social gatherings of real importance. Even at home the boys' and girls' quarters and activities were kept well apart. As a result of such conditions, *both sexes had to find their social and intellectual pleasures and stimulation among and by themselves.* The unmarried male population, young and old, was forced to find all its athletic, esthetic, intellectual, and social stimulations, satisfactions, and companionships with males and chiefly in company with males. It is no wonder that strong and no doubt questionable male friendships, as well as some perfectly honorable ones, naturally developed in such an unnatural social arrangement.

These realities, of course, qualify the Platonic Socrates' discussion of the nature and function of Love (*i.e.,* the god of love) in the cosmic scheme. As usual, Plato "winds himself into the subject like a serpent"

71

through a statement of Socrates' covering some twenty pages of Greek text. It is too long to present in its entirety; the best that space and reader patience will allow is an abstract of what Socrates says.

After Socrates and his host Agathon conclude that love is really the love of beauty; that love is always yearning and in love with what it lacks but does not yet possess; and that it loves but does not yet possess beauty, wisdom, and the good, Socrates turns to a recital of the instruction concerning the mysteries of love he had received from Diotíma, a highly clairvoyant priestess from Mantinéa. In paraphrase:

> As you suggested, Agathon, we must first explain just who and what sort of being Love is and second, what he is interested in accomplishing in the world. I had expressed to Diotíma my belief that Love was surely a great god, and a beautiful one. She, however, readily proved to me that he was not a god, and was neither beautiful nor good; he really lacked and yearned to possess both of these qualities —which any divinity would have to possess to be a god.
>
> Well, if Love is not a god, I said, what, pray is he, a mortal? Not at all, she said! He is a great Spirit [*i.e.*, a semi-divine being, *since his mother was a mortal and his father an immortal*], and, like everything else pertaining to spirit, he too is half human and half divine. Well, what is Love's function in the world and in life? Love, she answered, being both human and divine, *is an intermediate Spirit whose function is to mediate between gods and men, conveying to the gods men's prayers and sacrifices,*

*and interpreting to men the injunctions of the gods
and their rewards to men for the sacrifices they offer.*
For the gods themselves do not associate directly
with men but commune and converse with them,
both when they are awake and when asleep, only
through spirits, one of which is Love.

Now Love—which we have seen to be a great
intermediate Spirit mediating between the world of
mortality and the world of spirit—*is really love of
beauty, wisdom, and goodness in all their various
forms,* she said. *And Love's object in all these forms
is procreation in beauty,* whether it be in the realm
of the physical or in that of the spiritual. It
therefore expresses itself in many and various forms,
as it must, since there are numerous kinds of goodness,
wisdom, and beauty—beauty of body, deeds, character,
outlook, ideas, thoughts, etc.

The reason the generality of men fail to understand
Love and its extensive span of interests and activities,
she continued, is because they isolate one aspect
of its concern and give the name of love to that one
aspect only, assigning other names to Love's other
interests and purposes. They either forget or do not
realize that Love is the real source and authentic
inspiration, not of beauty, wisdom, and goodness
themselves, but of all creations, physical or spiritual,
conceived and brought forth *in* beauty, wisdom, and
goodness. Such procreations are the more numerous
because the generality of men are imbued with an
intense desire to bring to birth some creation,
physical or spiritual, of their own; for, by so doing,
they feel that they achieve a kind of immortality.

Remember also, Diotíma said, that different men

have different creative urges. The creative drives of some impel them toward physical procreation which incites them, in turn, to women, who satisfy their love and creative urges by bearing physical offspring for them. But there are other men who conceive spiritually—in their souls. These yearn quite naturally to bring forth such creations as the soul naturally begets and brings forth, namely wisdom, knowledge, and other potential human virtues. [I suppose Diotíma had in mind men who would, in time, bring forth such intellectual and spiritual offspring as have been produced by Moses, Socrates, Jesus of Nazareth, the world's greater poets, Michelangelo, Beethoven, Darwin, Einstein, *et al.*] When such men find themselves possessed from early youth by a desire to produce such spiritual, rather than physical, offspring, their first inclination is to seek out suitably beautiful surroundings and companionships so that they may, at the proper time, bring forth amid beauty their spiritual procreation. The first thing they look for and demand in those whom they seek as helpers and companions in their noble purposes are feelings and desires akin to their own, and emanating from noble and well-bred souls. If such persons happen to possess also a comely body, these spiritually "pregnant" persons will consider such comeliness a welcome, though not necessary, addition.

In an effort to instruct such associates, once they have been found, these spiritually-minded persons will converse much with them about human excellence, about the sort of person a good man should be and what practices he should pursue. After continued association with their acquired friends, contemplating them when they are with them and when they are not, and thus fixing in their minds and hearts the beauty inherent in these spiritual associates, those having conceived spiritually will bring to birth that which has been gestating all the while in their minds and souls. They thereafter nourish their spiritual progeny in conjunction with their noble-minded friends, with the result that a much more intimate and steadfast affection and partnership grows up between them than can develop between parents of physical offspring; for they nourish and share together a progeny more beautiful and immortal than ordinary parents share in. Surely anyone would prefer offspring such as these to any flesh-born children.

And now for the perfect revelation to which the love-mysteries so far discussed lead, exclaimed Diotíma! It is necessary, she said, for the one aiming rightly at this ultimate goal to begin, while he is still young, to contemplate well various specimens of physical beauty, and grow first of all to love one of them and beget in company with that one many discussions pertaining to what is beautiful. He will then come to see that the beautiful in any one physical body is kin to that in every other such body, and that genuine beauty in all bodies is one and the same. Once he realizes this, he will become a lover of all physical beauty and will relax any special love he may have for any particular example of beautiful young manhood, scorning it as too small and insignificant for his full devotion.

Our initiate into the mysteries of love will come by this time to perceive that beauty of soul is more to be honored than beauty of body. If therefore he encounters a male person fittingly beautiful in soul but endowed with only a moderate flower of youthful beauty, he will regard that as enough to be loved and cherished, and will seek to beget with him such talk and practices as will make young people better. He will thus be compelled to contemplate the beauty inherent in various customs and practices and will come to realize that all beauty is basically akin and to regard bodily beauty as of no great importance.

After considering the beauty in customary practices, he will be led to the sciences (arithmetic, geometry, music, etc.) to gaze upon their beauty. Viewing beauty by now as a single whole, he will no longer be content with individual examples,—like a slave lovingly content with a boy or some particular man or single practice—and thus slavishly become a mere worthless collector of trifles. He will turn rather to a contemplation of the vast sea of beauty now before him and, in his present abounding love of wisdom, thus beget many beautiful and magnificent sentiments and thoughts until, strengthened and spiritually enlarged by them, he will catch sight of the one unique knowledge of the following kind of beauty, to the explanation of which give now your most earnest attention, Diotíma said.

Whoever has been led this far into the mysteries of love, she said, and has observed them rightly and in proper order will, as he nears the end of his initiation, catch sight of something marvelous—the nature of true beauty, the very thing for which he has endured all his previous efforts. He will discover that this beauty is something eternal which neither increases nor wastes away but remains ever changeless to all who catch a true vision of it. He will see also that no form of physical beauty or reason or knowledge nor any creature or anything else on earth or in heaven can fully encompass and contain it. He will see that it exists in and of itself, in one eternal form. And even though it imparts a portion of itself to all other beautiful objects, which themselves increase and pass away, it itself remains neither more nor less than it was and never suffers any loss or damage.

Now when anyone, making his way through a proper love of boys begins to catch sight of this beauty, he is very near the end of his goal. And the right way for one to attain full initiation into the mysteries of love or be led through them by another is this: beginning from the fragments of beauty here on earth and using them as steps, he will ever climb upward toward eternal beauty, going from one beautiful object to two and from two to all individual forms of beauty, and from beautiful forms to beautiful practices, then from beautiful practices to beautiful knowledge until, from the various kinds of beautiful knowledge, he will finally arrive at that supreme knowledge which is related to nothing other than itself, and will come at last to know what beauty and goodness themselves, in all their fullness, are. [For the Greeks, the good, the beautiful, and the true are three names for one and the same entity. Also, this last long sentence is known as Plato's ladder to ultimate beauty and goodness.]

There, said Diotíma, if anywhere, my dear Socrates, is where man's life should be lived—beholding and contemplating true beauty in all its fullness. If you shall once see and apprehend this beauty, you will no longer think of it in terms of gold or raiment, beautiful children or young men, upon the sight of whom you and many others are now thrown into fits of ecstasy as you gaze on them in your continual association with them; and you are prepared to forego food and drink, if that were possible, provided you are allowed merely to gaze on and associate continually with them. What then, she said, are we to imagine it would be, if it should be possible for one to behold true beauty and goodness, clear, pure, undefiled, and untainted with flesh or colors and many other human trappings of little or no consequence but could see it as a single, undefiled entity in all its fullness?

Do you think, she said, that a person, living continuously with such beauty (and goodness) and gazing steadfastly on it, viewing it with that part of himself especially fitted for perceiving it rightly and fully, would be living a cheap and worthless life? Or don't you perceive, she said, that he alone, while gazing on such beauty with the faculty destined to render it visible in all its fullness, will be able to bring to birth, not mere shadowy reflections of human excellence since it is no mere shadowy reflection he is in contact with? He will rather bring to birth true human virtue and excellence, since true virtue and excellence is what he is in contact with. When therefore he has brought to birth and nourished to maturity this highest of all human virtues and excellence, he will then be dear to god and also immortal, if such is possible for man.

Such were Diotíma's instructions, Agathon, and they seem to me to be true.

In this sketch of what Socrates claimed Diotíma, the clairvoyant priestess of Mantinéa, taught him about love, I have adhered closely (using many of Mr. W. Hamilton's phrases)[9] to what, according to Plato, Socrates said. Further, I have presented the original material at considerable length for a reason: The subject is so touchy and easily misunderstood that I felt it was best— even necessary—to bring in all that might aid in understanding properly what Socrates was going to advocate.

There are two major elements in this presentation of Socrates that I have found helpful in coming to healthful and liberating terms with a very important aspect of life and living: First, the forceful way in which he raised the principal functions and possibilities of love so far above the level of just sexual inclinations and relations; and, second, his portrayal of love as the ultimate mediating Spirit, force, or power between man and the divine (*i.e.*, world of Spirit).

The latter concept was positively electrifying the moment I read it—*Love was an intermediate Spirit whose function was . . . to convey men's prayers and sacrifices to the gods, and to interpret in turn the injunctions and replies of the gods to men!* Here was a rather plain, though quite distant, similarity to one of the basic concepts inherent in the Gospels—that of a person, the veritable embodiment of love, as the mediator between man and the Deity. That it was *love* in both cultures—in one a god of love and all that pertained to it, and in the other an actively (so-called) divine embodiment of love—appeared to confirm my belief that genuine love has an indispensable role in all that is finest, most mature, and most enriching and ennobling in human relationships. The coincident idea was all the more arresting to me, since Greek culture is generally characterized as rational, while the early Hebrew culture, out of which the Christian outlook grew, is generally considered a spiritually intuitive one. Recognizing the similar ways in which two great cultures conceived of love kept me from turning in disgust from love as the most potent factor in achieving the best human relationships. Certainly the disgusting way love is abused and denigrated—I hope only temporarily—in so much of today's society is enough to restrain any perceptive person.

In the same passage in the *Symposium*, Socrates raised genuine love to a height completely above and beyond mere sexual interests. His view—and his reasoning—tended to confirm a long-held conviction of mine and strengthened it. Rather early in life, I had heard love identified with sex and sexual interest—something I instinctively disbelieved and later came to reject. Although I understood that people who loved each other naturally engaged in sexual relations at the proper time, that did not prove to me that sex and love were generically related or in any degree identical. I knew too many people who were ever ready and willing to engage in such relations without the slightest thought of anything that could be called love between the partners.

So, quite early in my maturing years I rejected for

myself a causative relationship between sex and love, and today's determined attempts to throw a halo around sex and even declare it the real matrix of love is, in my judgment, nothing short of treason to genuine love. The sex urge early seemed to me *chiefly an appetite* that needed to be satisfied from time to time just as other appetites do. Where real love is concerned, therefore, sex has seemed to me—not because of any frigidity—hardly more than a compelling concomitant to genuine love, much like healthful food, which one must have to live, is a compelling concomitant for whatever *quality of life and character* one will choose to honor and demonstrate in one's life and conduct. The basic purpose for sex was the survival of the species, and it is thus a necessary part of all creatures. The urge had to be powerful and pervasive enough in the human species to make its members willing to continue to undergo the care, trouble, and even peril involved from beginning to end in the process of producing and rearing offspring.

Admittedly, then, the feelings about sex and love that I brought to my reading of Socrates made me welcome his raising of love far above sex. To know that for a fifth-century Greek the word *Eros*, meaning love, could and did include in its meanings possible spiritual as well as the physical aspects of love was heartening indeed. It was the more impressive to me because this presentation came from Socrates, a heterosexual—he had three sons by his wife Xanthippe—who had proved himself, according to Alcibiades, thoroughly immune to homosexual temptations—and that, too, in a highly homosexual society.

What kind of love am I talking about? I cannot define it because years of effort have given me no definition that will comprehend its full measure. The best I can do is to offer a few of its characteristics that, if taken with sufficient charity and at something like face value, will suggest the kind of love in which I have long believed.

It is, first of all, a *supraphysical* love, transcending all physical concomitants involved in living a normal life of love. We accept now that anything that relates to a human being has some originating locus in the physical or psychological make-up. But the human animal is so "wonderfully made" and complex, and this transcendent love can show up in so many various aspects of outlook and conduct! Who can tell exactly where, if anywhere, in the bundle of complexities the originating matrix of the capacities for such love is located? Our ignorance in this matter is all but complete.

But whatever the originating matrix of supraphysical love, there are those—not many but some—who know from human experience that such love soon transcends every physical concomitant associated with it. If permitted, it becomes, as Diotíma said, a mighty spirit mediating between the true lover and his beloved. And such lovers experience this feeling more intensely as they give their total selves selflessly to each other.

The crowning argument, however, against this love's being innately identifiable with sex is what happens to such love when the sexual desires gradually fade from anticipation into reminiscence. Inevitably such a time comes when the desires wither into comparative non-existence, if one lives long enough, and the lovers of whom I speak can even say, "We have no excitable pleasure in them"; yet their supraphysical love falters not nor alters. Rather, it grows richer and deeper and settles into a fuller and more satisfying consolation. Such couples seek no divorce—legal or psychological—at this stage in their lives, but live even more firmly and securely drawn together. Their feeling is much like that expressed in Robert Burns's *John Anderson My Jo:*

John Anderson my jo, John,
We've climbed the hill together;
And many a jolly day, John,
We've had with one another;
Now we must totter down, John,
And hand in hand we'll go,
And sleep together at the foot,
John Anderson my jo!

So, to identify this love with sex, or to make it wholly or even chiefly dependent on sexual relationships, as so many present-day writers insist on doing or implying, is sad indeed and seems to me nothing less than unadulterated slander on genuine love.

For me, the ultimate matrix for this supraphysical transcendent love is "deep calling unto deep," a love that Mrs. Browning says is "for love's sake only." Even though conveniences will result from such love as inevitable concomitants, there is nothing of the "marriage for convenience" in it. It has no better or fuller reason for its existence than the *inestimable privilege* of being near the one loved, of having that one around, and of sharing in the loved one's total life—in its joys, sorrows, frustrations—all. It cheerfully gives everything to the person loved *just, and only, because that person is what he or she is.* It never deals in ulterior motives, nor deliberately resorts to those studied gifts, remembrances, and attentions with a meretricious aura around them. Gifts of this love are not validating evidences of such love—it needs none—but merely uncalculating promptings of "love for love's sake only."

Finally, it remains ever adequate for all the uncertainties each day may bring; it needs no courses in marriage—though other types very well may. This kind of love is its own best mentor for all the problems and crises that may arise.

However imprecise, these are the perceptions of the real character and attitudes of genuine love, as I have long conceived them. Granted, few couples have ever had the good fortune of experiencing this kind of love, which can be known only through experiencing or witnessing it. Robert and Elizabeth Browning doubtless knew it. Poe wrote of his Annabel Lee that the two had "loved with a love that was more than love," and whether or not he had experienced it, his recognition is there. I have heard that Madame Louise Homer and her husband Sidney were fortunate in this regard, and I am sure that a diligent search would uncover occasional instances of such love in every level of the world's societies.

There are also instances of a person's so loving, for some reason, an individual thoroughly unworthy and unresponsive. I myself witnessed for half a century a tragic example of such love heartlessly disregarded. Yet the love of this woman bore it out even to the end, maturing and growing richer in spirit all the while.

Because most of humanity has never known or seen such love demonstrated, there is a temptation to dismiss it as a kind of love "that never was on land or sea." Yet the fact that an individual has neither experienced nor witnessed such love is no proof that it doesn't exist; it proves only, as Berdyaev says, that his experience is limited. I would suggest, then, that no one readily dismiss the possibility of this transcendent love; keep it in mind as you read and as you move about in your daily living. You might encounter even yet an example of it. Remember, Socrates saw clearly, nearly 2400 years ago, how far fully-realized love transcends sex, even with an artificial halo around it. For this extensive and supporting insight, I shall ever be grateful to him.

XI Man the Measure of All Things

I doubt if anything encountered in the study of Greek affected my conception of our human predicament more radically than the discovery that the Greeks had apparently discerned correctly the inevitable subjectivity of all human knowledge and judgments, no matter how objective they might claim to be. *For nothing—literally nothing—can enter directly, just as it really is, into man's thinking and understanding.* Only after it has been properly interpreted by man can it be brought into man's outlook and conceptual framework, there to be related to his experience, his values, and his mental capacities. And it should be remembered *that any interpretation by man distorts to some extent the original integrity of the thing interpreted.* (When I hear a man in the pulpit say he doesn't interpret but just preaches the Bible, I always think: "Oh no, you don't. You preach *your interpretation*—a literal one perhaps, which is *still* an interpretation. This is all that you or anyone else can do.") For there is no situation or circumstance in which man can escape the "prison" of his finiteness and human limitations, and any judgment he renders is inevitably colored and affected, as it must always be, by his conditioning, by his interests, his outlook, and his point of view.

The pervasiveness of subjectivity is not stated by

the Greeks in such detail in any one work. Look at a single surviving statement by Protagoras of Abdera at the beginning of a work of his entitled *Truth* or *Refutatory Arguments*:

> Man is the measure of all things, of the things that are, that [or how] they are, and the things that are not, that [or how] they are not.

Unfortunately, this declaration is seldom quoted in full; all that is generally quoted is the first seven words. Also, the context that follows this statement has been lost. No one, therefore, can know exactly what Protagoras meant by it, and, as a consequence, it is variously interpreted. Some have held that he was trying to say that "each person's perceptions at any given moment are equally true for that person," while others have supposed Protagoras meant that objects do not exist except while they are being perceived by someone. I have also heard religionists argue that this declaration by Protagoras was simply Greek glorification of man and an expression of the Greek, highly anthropocentric culture.

Now we know that the Greeks did have much to say or imply about man's indomitable spirit and extensive achievements. Prometheus' long recital in Aeschylus' *Prometheus Bound*, detailing man's triumphs over his environment (lines 436 ff.); Sophocles' choral paean in his *Antigone*, praising man's restless and resolute cunning, which had overcome all his environmental obstacles and enemies except death (lines 332 ff.); and Theseus' lecture to Adrastus in Euripides' *Suppliants* (lines 196 ff.), on the blessings made available to man by the gods and the miserable mess made by man's misuse of them—all these testify to the high esteem in which man and his awesome mental and inventive powers were held by the Greeks. It is small wonder then that man with his frailties and wondrous possibilities constitutes the chief subject of Greek literature, since the Greeks seem to have been the earliest people to discern the fuller powers of the human mind and the first to envision the extensive role man could play in managing, changing, and controlling his life and environment.

But the praise and glorification of man and his possibilities do not mean, as some who comment on Protagoras' statement imply, that the Greeks considered man the ultimate being in importance in the universe. Greek authors from Hesiod and Pindar through Plato and Cleanthes' reverential hymn to Zeus mentioned earlier—pages 61–63—have too much to say about gods, beneficient spirits, the unwritten laws of god that are from evermore, and even about an all-seeing, ever-watchful, sin-avenging deity who cannot be thwarted or escaped, for anyone to claim legitimately that Greek civilization was anthropocentric *only*. The frequency with which Pindar, Aeschylus, Sophocles, and Plato speak of God or some remote, invincible, and mysterious presence in the offing with which man must always reckon or suffer the consequences should be ample proof, to any thoughtful reader, of the absurdity of such a claim.

So Greek civilization was not only man-centered. It was deity-centered also, though not to the extent the Hebrew culture was. And we may well be grateful that

Greek culture was not as deity-centered as the Hebrew; for the Greeks could hardly have shown the cultural and creative ingenuity they did, if they had been as priest-controlled as were the Hebrews. One important difference between these two deity-centered civilizations is seen in the manner in which each approached the God-man problem. The Greek approach was from knowledge up (the inductive method), whereas the Hebrew approach was from preconception down (the deductive method). Sir Livingstone[10] says quite correctly that, for the Greeks, God was a conclusion derived from their investigations and studies, whereas for the Hebrews, God was the major premise from which everything was viewed first of all by them.

But, all these matters aside, what concept was Protagoras most likely trying to make clear in his famous dictum? I have long felt that he was simply saying that whatever judgment man makes and whatever value he places on anything is made and evaluated from the standpoint of its value and use (or lack of use) to man. May not Protagoras very well have seen that man, just as any other creature capable of judging and evaluating, was compelled, by the very nature of things, to make his judgments and evaluations from the point of view of the worth and help that whatever he happened to be judging or evaluating might have for him and his kind? Xenophanes, a generation or so earlier, had said much the same thing in his comment about the various forms various animals would give to their gods, if they could form gods. And Sextus Empiricus (third century A.D.) held that man was doomed, by the very nature of things, to be himself the *criterion* and standard for any and all judgments he might make. Sextus argued further that men took hold only of those aspects of matter their condition enabled them to seize upon. Whatever is judged by man to be good or bad, beautiful or ugly, is thus judged to be so from man's, and from no other being's, point of view. Therefore, whatever is interpreted and evaluated by man is inevitably interpreted and evaluated on the basis of its advantage or disadvantage to man. And no matter how strenuously man may try to project his thinking and feelings unconditionally outside himself, his interests, standards, and values inevitably agree with his projected thoughts and feelings, showing that all human judgments and evaluations *are inevitably subjective*. There is, therefore, no such thing as a fully objective decision or conclusion; there are only more objective and less objective ones.

Protagoras' famous declaration seems to me to be somewhat reinforced by a fragment of one of Protagoras' contemporaries, Gorgias of Leontini in Sicily. Of this work, entitled *On Not Being or Concerning Nature*, only a long extract dealing with three theses maintained by Gorgias has survived. His theses were: that nothing exists in and of itself; if it did, it could not be known by man; and if it could become known to man, it could not be communicated. Here also, no one can know exactly what Gorgias had in mind. According to Sextus Empiricus, he appears to have tried to prove these theses by what appears to be the sheerest kind of logic chopping and logical squeezes. As a result, it is impossible to be sure just what he means by all this fancy logicality.

Rightly or wrongly, Professor Gonzalez Lodge ventures an interpretation of these theses, in the Introduction to his edition of Plato's *Gorgias*.[11] Professor Lodge says that what Gorgias attempted to prove was the impossibility of objective existence or the knowledge of such existence, and that, should man obtain knowledge of such existence, man would be unable to impart such knowledge to others by means of words. That is to say: Nothing exists or can be perceived to exist objectively in this world, or, if it does, man has no way of dealing with it; for whatever of reality becomes known to any living organism, including man, has to make itself known to that organism through the mist and fog of that organism's own particular limitations, values, and response-capabilities. *Consequently, by the time any portion of what is genuine reality becomes intelligible to man, it is no longer pure, objective reality but a modified version of it.* In like manner, if reality could become known to man in pure, objective form, his only means of communicating it to others would be through subjective human language that, as Tennyson observed, "half reveals and half conceals" the reality within. If this is a correct interpretation of Gorgias' theses—which I suspect it is—Gorgias' work seems to complement quite well the explanation given above of Protagoras' statement.

But if the inevitable subjectivity of all human concepts and knowledge is what Protagoras had chiefly in mind when he wrote his statement, the Platonic Socrates seems to have misunderstood his meaning (*Theaetetus*

161 ff.). He appears to have concluded that Protagoras' declaration meant only that however any part of reality appeared to an individual *that was the way it really was for him*. By extension, one person's conception of things becomes as true as any other person's; his might be *better* than another's but no truer. For Socrates, then, if each man's conception of wisdom was to be the best and the true one for him, why should anyone pay another to teach him wisdom? Since Protagoras advertised himself as a teacher of wisdom, among other things, Socrates wondered if Protagoras had not been joking when he wrote his famous dictum making man the measure of all things, of the things that are, that (or how) they are, and of things that are not, that (or how) they are not. Plato's discussion sounds a bit captious, which, in the light of his well-known dislike of sophists, it may well be. Plato must have known that Protagoras could readily have told Socrates why he made man, rather than a swine or any other animal, the measure of all things. Certainly, no one, not even one with only ordinary powers of comprehension, would make the measure of all things for man anything *less* than the most perceptive creature known.

Plato strikes out at Protagoras' dictum in his last work, the *Laws* (716c) by exclaiming that God, rather than man, should be the measure of all things for man. Yet, if all Protagoras intended his declaration to show was that all of man's knowledge and judgments are inherently and necessarily subjective and not objective, he could have readily replied to Plato's remark: "Exactly so. But what God?" It would have to be God as man can best conceive him; for that is the only God man can really "know." In this, therefore, as in the rest of life's aspects, man remains the measurer. There is no escape. Man's conception of the Deity may very well grow and be refined, as it generally does, *even though the Deity remains changeless.* The Deity of the Old Testament shows such growth in conception, and so also does the Greek conception of Zeus, though not to the same extent.

In sum, nothing can enter man's thinking until it is interpreted, and man must inexorably make all his interpretations from the standpoint of man or from man's conception of things. Nor has man any escape, in this world, from doing so. That, and chiefly that, it seems to me, is what Protagoras saw and was trying to make clear in his memorable statement.

XII Vengeance Not Confined to Sick Minds

Despite their great faith in reason and their devotion to it, the Greeks were apparently aware that the mind, with all its reasoning powers, was *not* the ultimate arbiter of human conduct. They saw something deeper and more imperious in man that could override his reasoning powers and bend them to its will without the health of the individual's mind being impaired in any way. According to the Greeks, this autonomous something in man, which they generally described as a demonic presence, could at times be actually good but was most frequently harmful, as it is considered today.

Such a demonic presence seems to me to account most rationally for certain vicious manifestations in human conduct. The evolutionary theory of the creation of man presages the survival of a demonic element in every person. Like every other inheritance, this demonic element seems to survive in degrees of intensity that vary by the individual. Most people eschew it and control it; but some others seem to find the element so attractive that they yield quite readily and rationally to its falsely promised satisfactions.

One of the deeper and more appealing demonic urges in man is one of the most insidious: the propensity to vengeance. Because it often masquerades as an instrument of justice, while being, in fact, a form of retaliation, vengeance has been responsible for some of the most heinous crimes in the history of man. It can be engineered by a single individual against an individual or against an entire class of people, and also by one group against another group.

The burden of this presentation, however, is not so much vengeance per se. It is intended, rather, to show that *not all instances of vengeance are the result of sick minds*—that easy oversimplification that confronts us so often today. To extend the sick-mind theory beyond all reasonable discretion—as it seems to me is being done—is about as uncritical as the old practice of attributing all evil conduct to something called the Devil. Some, perhaps most, schemes for vengeance issue from sick minds and spirits. But the Greeks appear to have believed that not *all* vengeance did.

With this preamble out of the way, let's look at an objective description of the lengths to which the democratic and oligarchic factions throughout Greece went in their efforts to implement vengeance against each other. One outbreak of this vindictive rivalry happened on the island of Corcyra (modern Corfu) in 427 B.C., the fourth year of the Peloponnesian War. Thucydides, the best-known historian of this war, describes the outbreak and generalizes his description in such a way as to imply that similar outrageous conduct occurred in other parts of Greece. In sections 82–3 in Book III of the *History of the Peloponnesian War*, Thucydides describes the situation:[12]

> There fell upon the cities during this period of faction and sedition many dreadful experiences, such

as happen and always will happen as long as human nature remains the same. . . . For factious violence ran its course throughout the cities of Greece, . . . and the invention of new schemes and devices went to exceeding lengths, as the excessive cunning of the attacks and monstrous forms of vengeance showed.

The generally accepted meaning of words as they related to deeds was changed at will to fit each man's conception of right. Reckless daring was called devotion to one's party, and prudent hesitation was branded as specious cowardice. Moderation was declared a cloak for unmanliness. To exhibit an understanding of all situations was an excuse for not acting in any. Frantic vehemence was accounted the part of a man, whereas deliberation which considered personal safety was thought to be a specious pretext for shirking. The storming firebrand was the one trusted, and anyone opposing him was always suspected. To form a plot and execute it was a mark of intelligence, but to suspect one indicated still greater acumen. Whoever insisted upon plans free from plots was called a disrupter of the party who was panic-stricken before the enemy. In short, that man was praised who beat to the draw one ready to do some evil, as he too was lauded who urged to evil one who was not yet planning evil.

The tie of blood became more foreign to one than party loyalty, which was more ready to proceed without pretext to any boldness. For party-clubs and alliances were made not for aiding established laws, but for overreaching others contrary to such laws. In fact, faith among party members was grounded in a common lawlessness rather than upon any regard for divine law. Favorable statements by an enemy in power were never received in a generous spirit but with an eye to his deeds and affairs. To get vengeance on another was more important than to keep free of injury. If oaths of reconciliation were anywhere accepted, they were temporary; for, being forced upon each party by some exigency of the moment, they lasted only as long as neither party had help from elsewhere. And the one who first caught the other opportunely off guard and was the first to resort to boldness enjoyed his revenge the more because it was gotten through trust rather than through open enmity; for by such a course of action he was assuring himself of safety, and, by getting the upper hand through deception, he was gaining also the prize for superior intelligence. Men found that villainy was considered a mark of skill and shrewdness more readily than disdain of these was thought a mark of goodness. They were ashamed of the latter but gloried in the former.

The cause of all this was government based on greed and ambition, together with the party zeal arising from it, and from men cast in factious rivalry. For the leaders in the various cities, each using fair-sounding phrases and declaring themselves devoted servants of the common good, had as their aim to capture as their prize all that pertained to the common good. Since each was struggling in every way to gain mastery over the other, they went to the most terrible lengths in their daring and to greater extremes in vengeance, considering neither any limits of justice nor the welfare of the state, but determining everything by what happened to please at the time; and having gained power either by violence or by an unjust vote of condemnation, they were ready to sate the contentiousness of the moment. The result was that neither side paid any regard to religious feelings or scruples; and he was most commended who accomplished some odious deed through speciously deceptive language. Moderate and neutral citizens were destroyed by both parties, either because of their refusal to join in the struggle, or through envy at their surviving.

Thus it was that every sort of character debasement became established in Greece through factious violence; and guileless forthrightness . . . was laughed out of existence and disappeared. Mutual hostility of feeling, combined with distrust, was triumphant and widely prevalent. For there was no language strong enough and no oath terrible enough to afford a basis for reconciliation; and all those in power, convinced of the hopelessness of securing any certain basis for confidence, were unable to trust any one and devoted themselves to precautions against being wronged. . . .

Here we have a discriminating and dispassionate statement of what can happen to ordinary people when they give themselves over to factious rivalry and to the cunning plans that vengeance naturally engenders. The demonic nature appears to take over their feelings, along with their reasoning processes, and draws them to its will and purposes. The ultimate arbiter for man's conduct thus becomes something deeper than normal feelings or the most competent reasoning powers. The Hebrews apparently identified the presence of a deeper control, which they referred to as one's heart. "Guard your heart with all diligence; for out of it flow the well-springs of life" is their admonition (Prov. 4:23).

Whenever man's deeper inner self really "sets its 'heart'" on anything, the mind, together with its reasoning powers, appears to renounce its function of guide and director, and stands ready to aid and abet this deeper inner self in whatever it has "set its heart upon." This seems to me the lurking pitfall that awaits all who would rely *only* on their reasoning powers as the single guide for all their plans and purposes. For it seems clear that the mind, even with all its superb competence and powers, is not in all cases the *ultimate* arbiter for human conduct. This is especially true where one's most treasured interests, purposes, and possessions are at stake.

Thucydides' account graphically depicts the general character and ubiquitous chaos that resulted from an uninhibited amoral struggle for political power by the prevailing factions. The schemes of vengeance devised were fatal to all desirable character and social good feeling on both sides. It hardly seems reasonable to assert that all the leaders of these political factions were sick in mind, just as it would seem unreasonable to argue that all leaders of any two political parties are sick-minded.

But what about single individuals bent on vengeance? Is it possible for any person inordinately given to vengeance to be also a healthy-minded individual? The question can never be definitely answered, just as no one can really know or prove that all human conduct is wholly determined. About all that can be honestly done is to examine the available evidence and choose the conclusion that seems in all honesty to account in the most reasonable manner for what we have observed.

In my judgment, a healthy-minded individual *can* be vengeance-bound. The assumption that there is something demonic deep within man that, unless properly restrained and renounced *personally*, can issue into inhuman forms of vengeance through a healthily functioning mind, explains most reasonably the individual acts of vengeance that apparently issue from healthy minds.

Euripides portrayed Medea, in 431 B.C., as such a highly demonic woman who planned and executed her heartless vengeance through a shrewdly cunning and healthily functioning mind. Little in Greek life and culture would lead Euripides to view Medea's deed otherwise, for the Greeks regarded vengeance not only as natural and honorable but even as a duty for all who had been wronged in any way. It was encouraged rather than discouraged. For Euripides there was nothing unnatural about Medea's vengeance, except its enormity. Also, the Greeks had no scientific basis for any theory of human sick-mindedness.

Let's look now at the play so that you can decide for yourself what Euripides had in mind in his presentation.

Jason had set out from Iolcus in northern Greece to reclaim the treasured Golden Fleece from the king of Colchis at the eastern end of the Euxine Sea. The king's daughter Medea, a powerful sorceress, apparently fell passionately in love with Jason the moment she saw him, and she determined to help him obtain the fleece and also to save him from the murderous plans of her father. In return for her help, Jason took her back to Iolcus in northern Greece and made her his wife. In time, she bore Jason two sons, which was the greatest boon a wife could bestow on a Greek husband. (Remember how significant male heirs were in the Greek society. A male heir assured the husband of someone to perpetuate his name, which meant, in turn, that he would have someone to inherit his property and thus keep it within the family. Finally, the husband would have someone to give him the most authentic burial possible—an act upon which the Greeks laid great stress.) Moreover, Medea, through her magical powers, helped Jason to avenge the slaying of his (Jason's) father by Pelias, his uncle. For this, she, Jason, and their two sons were exiled to Corinth, where Jason, weary of being married to a foreigner by whom he could never beget royal children, planned to desert Medea and then marry Glauce, the daughter of Creon, king of Corinth.

Euripides presents Medea as a woman who could absorb much, but Jason's acts had gone beyond the limit of her endurance. *The one thing she could not and would not tolerate was to be mocked and triumphed over by anyone whom she regarded as an enemy.* So, in return for this betrayal by Jason, whom she now regards as an archenemy, Medea determines to strip Jason of everything dear or of advantage to him. She resolves therefore to kill the new bride and the bride's father, and then slay her two sons by Jason. She would thus deprive Jason of his children, his royal bride, and his hopes for royal offspring; his name would thus die, and, without proper burial at the hands of his heirs, his entrance into the next world would be difficult. How she could more completely strip Jason of all he most cherished and was working to obtain can hardly be imagined.

The brutality of Medea invites our writing her off simply as someone devoid of all human feeling. But as Euripides portrays her, she is not totally inhuman. You can detect this in her farewell speech to the children, which I would like to translate for you so you can make your own decisions. Here is the setting: Medea's sons have just returned from delivering to the prospective bride a robe and crown sent by Medea under the guise of being a reward for a hoped-for reprieve from exile for which the children were to ask. The gifts had been treated with a drug that body heat would activate into flames; they could neither be shaken off nor snatched from the wearer's body. Further, anyone taking hold of the victim's body could never free himself but would himself be slain, as the prospective bride's father actually was when he tried to save his daughter.

Now, it is when the children have returned from carrying these gifts that Medea, knowing that the poison in her gifts would work, confronts her final task of killing her children. This act would complete her vengeance on Jason. Notice how rational she is and how she wrestles with her maternal feelings. Notice also that it is *her inability to endure mockery at the hands of her enemies* that finally drives her to the deed. When the children are brought in, she speaks to them as follows:

"Oh children, children, henceforward you will have a home and city in which, after leaving wretched me, you will dwell bereft forever of me, your mother. But, as for me, I shall go an exile to another land before I have had my joy in you and seen you reach your state of happiness—before I have adorned your bride and nuptial bed, and held aloft for you the wedding torch. O wretched one that I am, and *all because of my own stubborn will!*

"It was in vain that I suffered and was racked with pain as I endured the pitiless pangs of child-birth. I once—ah wretched me—had many a hope that you would care for me in my old age, would shroud me well and lay me out when I had died—a boon much craved by mortals! But as things are, that cherished hope is gone, yes gone forever! For I, deprived of you, shall lead a life both grievous for me and painful. And you will no longer behold your mother with your dear eyes, going, as you are, to another kind of life.

"Ah me! ah me, my children! Why gaze on me like that? Why cast on me that final smile? Alas! What am I to do? My heart fails me, Corinthian women, as I look into the bright eyes of these children. I cannot do the deed! Farewell to all my former plans and schemes! I'll take my children from this land. Why should I, while trying to punish their father through bringing evils on them, bring on myself woes twice as great? I will not do it. Farewell to these schemes of mine!

"But what is this now coming over me? Am I to

let my enemies go unpunished and become thereby
an object of their mockery? No! Never! I must dare
the deed. What a coward I was even to admit
relenting words into my thoughts! Into the house, my
children! [The children depart.] And let whoever
thinks he should not be present at my offering see to
it that he isn't; for I will not allow my hand to falter.

"Yet don't my heart; don't do the deed! Spare the
children, wretched one, and let them live! Living with
us in exile, they will cheer you, heart of mine.

"No, heart of mine! By the avenging fiends below
in Hades, *I will never hand my children over to their
enemies to mock them and insult them.* Already
they have now been doomed to die, and, since they
have, I, I who bore them, will slay them; for their
doom is fixed and there is no escape.

"Already the royal bride has on her head the crown
I sent her and is writhing now in the robe I gave her.
That I know clearly. So, since I now shall fare along
the wretched path of exile while sending the children
on a path more wretched still, I would speak to
you again, my children. [The children are again
brought in.] My children, give your mother your right
hand to kiss. O dearest hand, O lips most dear to me!
O noble form and features of my children! May
happiness be yours—happiness there at least—since
your father has deprived you of your happiness here. O
sweet embrace, soft flesh and fragrant breath of
children! Go! Go! Be gone! I can no longer look on
you! For I am overcome of evil. *I see and understand
the sort of evil deed I am about to do. But angry
passion, the cause of direst evils to mortals, has*

104

overcome my sober, temperate thoughts." (My italics throughout.)

Such is Medea's soliloquy. Notice how lucid and rational she is. And if vengeance was ever sweet, it seems to have been sweet indeed to her. For when the messenger enters to announce that the princess and her father are dead, she coolly says, "Tell me how they died; and don't hurry." Apparently she wishes to enjoy the greater satisfaction from her vengeance on them and indirectly on her faithless husband. Also, when Jason enters and, after learning of the children's death, upbraids her at some length, Medea, from the safety of the hoisted chariot sent by her father, the sun-god, calmly says to him, "It was not destined for you to scorn my couch and pass a joyful life while mocking me. Nor was your royal bride or Creon, who arranged for you another marriage, destined to drive me, with impunity, from this land. So, call me a lioness or Tyrrhenian Scylla, if you like. But *I have wrung your heart, as it was right I should.*" When Jason reminds her that she too will grieve and suffer for this loss, "I know," she says. "Yet *it eases my pain to know that you can never mock me.*" "You have slain the children," Jason says. "And plunged you into ruin," is Medea's cold reply.

Such are the lengths and callous conclusions to which an unbridled devotion to an inordinate desire for vengeance can lead even a physically unimpaired and rationally functioning mind. Was Anne Lindbergh's observation true, when she declared that the intellectual is always betrayed in the end, because the mind with its reasoning powers generally fails one just when the individual most needs its most objective guidance—when some inordinate desire is pressing most inordinately upon him? Are there circumstances or a point at which a person's rational powers can and will renounce their role of devil's advocate and become a rationalizing ally, helping the person formulate rational justifications for doing what he then most desires to do?

These are some of the questions that have confronted me as I have studied the *Medea*. How much truth they contain no one can know beyond question; but they appear to me to contain enough truth to give one pause—as they have given me many times. They have constrained me to ask many times: Is this bona fide reasoning or merely obsequious rationalizing? As I see it, various literatures contain too many examples of uncontrolled vengeance and its direful results for such questions as these to be ignored or brushed aside and such conduct treated as an instance of temporary mental aberration for which the persons involved have little or no responsibility.

Here again I cheerfully acknowledge my gratitude and indebtedness to those keen-minded Greeks for helping me realize what continually harbored hatred and persistently pursued vengeance always do to the characters of those who harbor and activate such feelings in their lives and conduct. Their presentations have been a constant warning to me not to give place to these passions in my life and thinking. They further helped me to see more clearly that St. Paul was doubtless right in insisting that vengeance was not a human prerogative.

"Vengeance is mine; I will repay, saith the Lord," is Paul's statement (Rom. 12:19). The Greek authors reinforced anew my feeling that any society, being more and more crowded together as ours is, has no need for anything whose nature is to divide and destroy as hatred and vengeance do.

As we close this discussion, three essentials should be remembered and kept in mind. The first is the very close kinship between vengeance and retaliation, one of the earliest and most deeply imbedded urges in man. We meet it in the early law, "An eye for an eye and a tooth for a tooth." We hear it in children as they say, "He hit me first." And we listen to it as we hear parents exhort their children "to give him as good as he sends." If the difference is not settled to the satisfaction of both parties because one has an advantage over the other, revenge will seem the just and natural way to even the score. Revenge will thus appear to have an aura of justice about it.

Note, too, how closely vengeance seems to be allied with a tendency to hate. Genuinely loving natures seldom resort to vengeance.

Finally, remember that what is said in this presentation is not intended even to imply that man is born congenitally evil. He seems to me to be born both *potentially* good and *potentially* evil. Which *potential* he will develop as he grows to maturity depends ultimately on him—on which potential he sides with and encourages by the choices he makes and the ideals he clings to in his purposes and conduct.

Much of this problem was clarified for me by the Greeks.

XIII An Exhortation to Humility

The Greeks had two aphoristic sayings that have proved, in my case, a good antidote for a prideful ego. I would like therefore to pay homage to these two Greek sayings, although modern writers and publicists would doubtless damn them as worthless clichés.

Incidentally, this hue and cry against clichés per se puzzles me, for don't clichés do for written statements what words do for concepts—state them as clearly and precisely as possible? If that is true, are they not only needed but necessary for the clearest and most precise communication? To repudiate clichés as a legitimate instrument for acceptable communication would be, it seems to me, to renounce one of our best means for transferring ideas as concisely as possible from person to person. I see no reason arbitrarily to deny the use of many of the best statements yet devised of many of our noblest and most civilized moral and spiritual truths.

If I understand what these objectors to clichés mean by the term, most of the Ten Commandments and the Beatitudes would have to be considered clichés. And we would have to abandon—which I am not prepared to do—phrases that, when used properly, mean so much:

God is love.
Keep your heart with all diligence.
The unexamined life is not livable for a man.
Bear one another's burdens.
God fulfills himself in many ways.
God will work with you but not for you.
No man is an island to himself.
The old order changes yielding place to new.
Men may rise on stepping stones of their dead selves.
The envious man is his own enemy.
Love of money is a root of all evil.

On the basis of the present attitude toward clichés, these and countless other statements of timeless truths would have to be considered inadmissible in acceptable writing today, as would numerous proverbs, maxims, and epigrams from the world's literature.

There are, of course, untrue clichés and those that have to be interpreted if their true meaning and application are to be understood. "Power corrupts men and absolute power corrupts absolutely" is an example of a cliché that is untrue and a slander on power. *Power never corrupted anyone.* It can only arouse and bring into the open as much potential corruption as is already latent in the person in power—something latently present in all but the choicest individuals. Who can truthfully say that power corrupted Abraham Lincoln or Robert E. Lee or Dwight Eisenhower?

Of course, there are clichés so ambiguous in meaning and application as to demand explicit interpretation in order to be properly judged. Remember: "Spare the rod and spoil the child," meaning, "If you spare the rod you will spoil the child"? Now does that mean use the rod regularly to beat the devil out of the child and thus save him from being spoiled? Or does it simply mean if you spare (*i.e.*, never use) the rod you will spoil the child? Both of these policies are negative; so here is a cliché that is not only ambiguous but downright bad, certainly in the case of most children. Still, I see no sufficient reason for condemning the use of any and all clichés. Many are true, excellent, and highly useful, when used properly as other things are.

But all this comment aside, the two Greek aphorisms I have in mind in this presentation are these: "Know thyself," and "Keep sober and remember to distrust." Like many Greek aphorisms, exactly what each of these statements meant to its originators is not entirely clear. The chances are very great that they each meant different things to different Greeks. Let's look first at the one whose message to each person is: Know thyself.

We do not know the author of this exhortation or when it was first written. Diogenes Laertius (third century A.D.) attributed the saying to Thales of Miletus, a mathematician and philosopher who predicted an eclipse of the sun in 585 B.C. We know also that the expression was carved on the temple of Apollo at Delphi, an indication of its prominence among the Greeks and of the respect with which the idea was held.

A general exhortation such as "Know thyself" can obviously be given a wide span of meanings, as doubtless happened in this case. One of the more widely held meanings for it seems to have been: Know (*i.e.*, remember) that you are mortal and conduct yourself accordingly. The Greeks have much to say, in one form or another, about man's propensity to act as though he were supramortal, superior to the natural laws and limitations applicable to ordinary men. Clearly, they thought too much wealth and power could easily induce men to become arrogant and even scornful of the gods. Such men as Creon in the *Antigone* and Pentheus in the *Bacchae*, both of Thebes, were examples of this arrogance. There were honors too high for man, as Agamemnon acknowledged when he asked his wife Clytemnestra not to honor him as a god when she was welcoming him home from Troy.

The Greeks worked out a threefold pattern to account for the punishment they thought they saw visited on overweeningly proud and arrogant men. The first element in this pattern was *koros*, that wearisome disgust that often creeps over one who finds himself possessed of unusually great wealth and power. More frequently than not, *koros* leads naturally to the second element in this pattern devised by the Greeks, which is *hybris*, that arrogance which causes a man to take neither god nor man into account. It can even cause a man to defy both. But once the victim of *hybris* has scorned the will and power of the gods, Ate, the goddess of infatuation and ruin—the third element in this punitive pattern devised by the Greeks—enters secretly into all his plans and purposes. She accomplishes her destructive purpose by so confusing the arrogant victim's interpretative powers and judgment that he will misinterpret his courses of action. What he will then choose, thinking it is good for him, will prove ruinous for him, and what would really be good for him he will reject because he will think it is bad for him. By this device Ate easily inveigles him into utter ruin. It was such ruin of the wealthy and powerful, when it could have been avoided by proper restraint and conduct, that apparently impressed the Greeks; and this "trinity" of *koros*, *hybris*, and *Ate* was the explanation they worked out to account for such unnecessary ruin. It thus appears to have been the Greek way of saying to those who were greedy for wealth and power: Know yourself, and remember that you are mortal.

Moreover, according to the Greeks, their gods, who in early times were more powerful than men but not vastly different from them, were unwilling for mortals to be on a level with themselves in happiness, affluence, and power. So they wanted men to remember that they were mortal and to avoid any competition with gods in wealth, happiness, and power. "Know thyself" was an invitation to the Greeks to know also their limitations and live both with their limitations and within them. In other words, this maxim was an appeal for continuous self-examination.

A special human weakness to which this admonition would apply is human pride. References to this human failing, either by inference or direct statement, are met in every period of Greek literature. (See Professor David Grene's *Man in His Pride* (1950), based on his interpretation of the writings of Thucydides and Plato.)[13]

As the Greeks viewed the matter, there were two

forms of human pride that the gods would never allow to go unpunished: overproud utterances or deeds. The Greeks developed a technical phrase, *epos mega*, for an overproud utterance. The phrase meant literally a great word, but it meant, in fact, *too* great a word for man to utter.

A passage from Sophocles' *Ajax* (lines 758 ff.) will illustrate Greek feeling in this matter as well as furnish examples of the Greek *epos mega*:

> Men overproud and foolish, said the prophet,
> Fall ruinously crushed by grievous calamities,
> Whenever, being born a mortal man,
> They turn to thinking thoughts too great for mortals.
> Even so was Ajax, setting out from home,
> Discovered to be thus foolish, when his father
> Wisely said to him: "My child, strive always
> To prevail in battle; but do so always
> After seeking help from heaven."

But foolish Ajax proudly said in answer:

> "Father, a worthless nobody could prevail
> With help from heaven; but I am persuaded
> That, without help from gods, I shall prevail
> And win a victor's glory."

There follows in this passage a second *epos mega* spoken by Ajax. When the goddess Athene was urging him to turn his murderous hands against the enemy, he uttered in turn to her these direful, blasphemous words:

> "Queen goddess, go and incite to battle
>   the rest of the Greeks;

For where I am stationed, our line will
    never break."

Sophocles provides another example of an *epos
mega* in his *Antigone* (lines 1039–41), a passage we discussed earlier. You will recall Creon, the king, had refused to allow Polyneices to be buried, and carnivorous
birds were preying on his body and, later visiting the
altars of the gods in Thebes, were polluting the altars of
the city. Teiresias, the chief seer of Thebes, comes and
urges Creon to have Polyneices buried and save the city
from pollution. To this Creon angrily replies that Polyneices would remain unburied, even if the eagles of
Zeus should pollute the throne of Zeus with Polyneices'
flesh.

The punishment for such prideful blasphemies apparently impressed the Greeks; for, even though the punishment was not always swift, it seemed to them sure.
For his impudent remark to Athene, Ajax was driven
mad by her and, in his madness, so disgraced himself
that he committed suicide after he came to his right
mind. Creon, through his stubborn impiety, was stripped,
through death, of his wife, his son, and his niece, and
was himself killed in a battle brought on by his refusal
to allow burial for the dead Argives. Remember what
Oedipus suffered soon after his prideful boast that he
would never be dishonored. The comment of the chorus
at the close of the play can be considered typical of
Greek feeling toward prideful statements of overproud
men. Here it is:

Look, dwellers in our native Thebes;
This is Oedipus, who knew the famous riddle

And was a man of power exceeding great. . . .
Therefore, look to man's final day
And count no mortal happy till you see
He has crossed the bounds of his existence
Free from pain and grief.

The last six lines of Jonson's *Sejanus* are singularly applicable to Greek feeling in this matter:

Let this example move the insolent man
Not to grow proud and careless of the gods.
It is an odious wisdom to blaspheme,
Much more to slighten or deny their power;
For whom the morning saw so great and high
Thus low and little before the even doth lie.

Along the same line, only more general, is Isabella's somewhat more cutting statement in Shakespeare's *Measure for Measure*, Act II, scene ii, lines 144 ff.:[14]

But man, proud man,
Dressed in a little brief authority,
Most ignorant of what he's most assured,
(His glassy essence), like an angry ape,
Plays such fantastic tricks before high heaven
As make the angels weep.

We have looked at two special aspects of "Know thyself," a need for a sense of place, of limitations and responsibilities in the scheme of things, and a need for recognition of the innate tendency to excessive pride with its direful results.

But this command was too general to be limited to any two aspects. As Miss Eliza Wilkins' volume *The Delphic Maxims in Literature*[15] shows, it could be, and was, applied by the Greeks to almost every phase of man's life and being in which he was ignorant. Moreover, in a culture that could produce the Platonic Socrates, we can be rather sure that there were Greeks for whom this injunction would mean a charge to discover and remember their human propensities, potentialities, and obligations both to themselves and to others and to realize in their lives and conduct their best impulses and possibilities. Such Greeks would likely see also in this aphorism an appeal to take cognizance of what kind of persons they actually were in their deepest inner selves—that part (the soul) which Socrates regarded as the real self. Socrates makes this clear in the dialogue *First Alcibiades* (sec. 124–35).

For Socrates "Know thyself" would seem to be a cosmic injunction to man to know that the most important part of himself (his soul) is immortal, and that man's most important task in life is to make and keep his soul as just and as free of evil as possible. In his defence before the Athenian court he cited that particular statement as a summary of his basic admonition, as a teacher, to the Athenians. He says in Plato's *Phaedrus* (230a) that he has no time to investigate myths, *because he must first find out about himself*: whether he is some intricate beast full of furious passion or a simpler and gentler creature, having within himself a modest share of some divine allotment.

This interpretation of the aphorism intrigued and encouraged me. It had long seemed to me that we are not born destined by nature to become good nor doomed by nature to become evil, but with only the *potential* for becoming predominantly one or the other, depending on which we really choose to become.

And Socrates seems to have believed that man had been endowed with the ability to choose and had been charged also with responsibility for the results of his choices, for choices seem to be neither wholly undetermined nor wholly determined. He appears to suggest this idea in Plato's *Republic* (617e), where he portrays Lachesis (one of the three Fates) as saying to the souls she is readying to be born: "No divinity is going to cast lots for you, but you are going to choose your tutelary divinity . . . and choose also the [kind of] life with which you will of necessity be conjoined. Virtue has no master; each of you, therefore, will have more or less of her in proportion as you honor or fail to honor her. So choose, remembering that any resulting blame belongs to him who chooses; for God in this is blameless." I wouldn't pretend to know what the full import of this passage would be for Greek thinkers; but I do know that it was of immense help to me in clarifying my own feeling about man's ability to make choices and his responsibility for doing so.

These are some of the specifics apparently demanded by this maxim, "Know thyself," that have proved helpful in my thinking, limited as it is. Certainly, this particular maxim has had a long history of influence in later literature. It became a favorite precept among the Stoics, and appears in connection with the concept of self-knowledge in some of the Christian Church Fathers.

It showed up later in the Renaissance and continued to receive consideration in Western European thought into the nineteenth century.

"Keep sober, and remember to distrust," the second maxim, can be dealt with more briefly. I did not need any admonition to keep sober, for I early concluded that I would not knowingly bring about any condition in my body that would cause or even allow me to act more foolishly than my limited abilities had already made inevitable. But the warning to "remember to distrust" was advice I very much needed, and it has proved immensely helpful to me. It appeared to me to be a clear admonition to keep an open mind and to remember that even our best thoughts and conclusions may be wrong or, at least, inadequate. It helped me to see that for a person to close his mind permanently on any subject would be to cut himself off from the help new knowledge might put at his disposal. In the light of this perception I decided therefore to take my morals, attitudes, motives, purposes just twenty-four hours at the time. So doing has enabled me to integrate into my thinking and purposes each newborn morning whatever new information and insights I had encountered the preceding day. (This is not as impossible as it sounds, since not every day brings relevant new knowledge or insights. Consequently, any morning I found myself without any new knowledge or insights to be built into the guiding lights I had lived by on the preceding day—and this happened frequently—I simply used for the new day the lights I had lived by on the preceding day.)

It is not easy for young people to accept a maxim

that bids the distrust of even youthful idealism with its yen for perfection because it may not be as final and perfect as it may seem. The easy thing is to say: Well, what is the use? Yet the demand of the maxim remains adamant for me. In this life, my task, as a responsible human being, is still to strive for the best information and the most reasonable insights I can acquire and then act on them, even though I realize they are not perfect and might not even be as good as they appear to me to be.

This I have tried to do, and in the process I discovered for myself that the only way for me to grow in knowledge was to act first of all on whatever knowledge I already happened to have, imperfect though it necessarily was. This could be done only on the basis of an open mind; and only thus could "knowledge grow from more to more," and life become fuller, richer, and immensely more rewarding even through perilous uncertainties. This outlook enabled me to see, as Professor H. J. Muller has said in his *The Uses of the Past*,[16] that "Our business as rational beings is not to argue for what is going to be but to strive for what ought to be, in the consciousness that it will never be all we would like it to be."

Two general precautions, however, should be kept in mind. The precept does not call on us to *so distrust that we are unable to act*. It asks only that we remember our inevitable fallibility and that everything in our world is ordained to be always changing and growing, sometimes for the better—and sometimes for the opposite, as Sophocles would add. Nothing therefore can be perfect. If it ever became perfect, it could not continue so.

Remember, too, that the distrust this maxim asks for is not to be based on personalities but on the consciousness of our human inability ever to obtain fully perfect knowledge. I wish our leaders today would seriously believe and heed this injunction and then urge us to do likewise.

XIV   *The Mean*

The idea of regular balance and proportion that characterizes nearly everything the Greeks created impresses itself on any observant person viewing the creations of the Greek Classical period. The general absence of impertinent excess or extravagance is readily noticeable. This quality is true of Grecian architecture, sculpture, and earthenware. Their literary forms—epic, lyric, tragedy, history, oratory, music and, to a less extent, their philosophy—and practically everything basic to their culture also reflected the Greek concern with the mean. It was chiefly in comedy and in some religious rites and practices, especially those connected with the god Dionysus and his worship, that excess and lack of restraint were fully condoned by the Greeks.

The instinct for proportion, proper measure, and balance as essential ingredients in whatever was to be beautiful was apparently arrived at early in Greek history. (Professor Paul Shorey, professor of Greek at the University of Chicago and the most widely read man in Western literature that I have ever known, used to say that Greek literature contained the best combination of the poetic and the rational that he had found in any European literature.) The expression "due measure is best in everything" occurs twice in Homer's *Odyssey* (7:310 & 15:71), and Hesiod has this exhortation:

"Observe due measure; for proper proportion in all things is best" (*Works and Days*, 694). But it is the latter part of the sixth century B.C. before we meet, in the *Proverbs* of Theognis of Megara (line 335), the classic Greek expression related especially to this idea of balance and proportion. The expression is *meden agan*, and meant "In nothing too much," *i.e.*, "Not too much of anything"—not even something good. Like the maxim "Know thyself," *meden agan* too was inscribed on the temple of Apollo in Delphi. It is found in Aeschylus, Sophocles, and Euripides, and four times in Plato. Aristotle refers to it twice in the second book of his *Rhetoric* (xii 14 and xxi 13–14). Miss Wilkins' *The Delphic Maxims in Literature*[17] further details the history of this expression through Latin literature, the Renaissance, and into the present time. *Meden agan* thus seems to have been even more popular than the maxim "Know thyself."

Meden agan is criticized by some because it says nothing about the opposite proportional imbalance "too little." Perhaps this balance was omitted because it would be so readily inferred by the Greeks that it did not need to be expressed. Or the Greeks may have felt strongly that *excess* rather than *deficiency* in action clearly seemed more prone to bring unpleasant consequences. This deficiency of the aphorism was remedied, however, by Aristotle, the master analyzer and logician of the fourth century B.C., when he deduced and defined his doctrine of "the mean," making it the logical device for achieving the highest human excellence. He went into this problem of the mean in considerable detail in book II (chapter vi, sec. 1–ix, 9) of his *Nicomachean Ethics*, a work named for his son Nicomachus who, while young, was killed in battle.

Aristotle first notes that the mean is of two kinds: an absolute mean, and a relative mean. The absolute mean applies to things and is always one and the same for everybody. It is the term used to describe one thing: the central point equidistant from the extremes of anything. Thus, the mean (point) between 1 and 100 would fall between 50 and 51. The constitution, feelings, actions, and reactions of the individual have nothing to do with locating the absolute mean of anything. This mean is already fixed by forces exterior to man, and all man has to do is discover at what point it has been fixed.

The *relative* mean, however, varies with each individual, for the individual's constitution, choices, feelings, emotions, and needs constitute the essential factor in determining the proper mean for himself. It is this relative (and not the absolute) mean that Aristotle is interested in throughout his discussion of the mean in his *Ethics*. To him, the mean is that amount of anything that is neither too much (excessive) nor too little (deficient) for the individual being considered. Each of us must therefore discover for himself his proper mean in the various aspects of living, if he is to realize in his life and conduct his full potential for human excellence.

The food-mean for manual laborers and for sedentary workers will be different, since their bodies demand different amounts of food for healthy bodies. The drinking-mean for a temperate drinker and an alcoholic is not the same. For an alcoholic the drinking-mean is said to be zero, whereas, for a temperate drinker, it will vary according to his physical condition and how vigorously alcohol affects his system. The relative mean will be different for a sensual and for a refined person. Aristotle says the mean for adultery and murder is zero.

As Aristotle analyzed the problem, actions and expressions of feeling in general had in them the possibility of excess, deficiency, and due measure in their implementation. Excess and deficiency were vices, and only the mean could claim to be considered virtue. Thus, there was only one way to be morally right, namely, by living and acting in all situations on the basis of the mean. But there were numerous ways to go wrong and thus fail in achieving moral excellence, which, in turn, meant that to realize in our conduct our full human potential for moral excellence is most difficult, if not impossible. For, if our feelings and actions are to eventuate in morally right conduct they must be felt and implemented "at the proper time, on the proper occasion, toward the right persons, for the right reason, and in the proper manner and measure." [18] To act and feel in this manner is to attain the mean and the highest state of moral excellence.

Human excellence or virtue thus turns out to be "a fixed disposition to make deliberate choices based on the mean relative to us, determined by reason, as a prudently wise man would determine it." [19] The middle state lies between two vices, one falling short of what is proper and the other exceeding it. But the mean itself is the highest and best state possible.

Yet there are actions and feelings that are incapable of having a mean, since they are wholly bad. Malice, envy, murder, adultery, injustice, profligacy, are examples. Any indulgence in such as these would be per se excessive and therefore wrong.

On the other hand, courage, justice, perfected self-mastery, and the like do not admit of excess or deficiency *since they carry within themselves their own due mean.* To modify such as these in any meaningful degree from that demanded by their own perfection would be to transmute them into something different from what they are. Most actions and feelings, however, are capable of being engaged in excessively, deficiently, or in accordance with due mean.

Aristotle recognized that his general definition of moral excellence (virtue) needed to be expressed in more practical detail to be serviceable. He therefore discussed several actions and reactions in detail as examples of what acting on the basis of the proper mean really involved. Here are three of the ten or twelve samples he detailed. (1) Regarding actions involving boldness and fear, overboldness was excess, courage was the mean, and cowardice the defect. (2) Regarding the spending and dispensing of money, prodigality was excess, proper liberality the mean, and penuriousness the defect. (3) In regard to anger, irascibility was the excess, proper indignation the mean, and apathy or indifference the defect.

Aristotle's attempt to expand into a rational mold the simple Greek maxim "In nothing too much" and cast it into a kind of syllogistic framework is only partially successful. It is easy, however, to see, just as Aristotle did, that such a generalized rational partitioning of human actions and reactions is too full of pitfalls to be a very helpful guide. How far, for example, would a properly courageous person have to move from the mean of courage for his action to be considered rash instead of courageous? How far would a discerningly liberal man have to depart from the mean relative to handling money before he would have to be considered penurious? At what point in a person's reaction to his feeling of anger must he be considered irascible, properly indignant, or apathetic?

So, while declaring the mean praiseworthy and the extremes reprehensible in all matters Aristotle took pains to point out that it was difficult indeed to discover the mean in actions and feelings. It is easy, he says, to become angry, or dispose of money; *but to be angry or to rightly dispose of money to the right person, in the proper amount, at the right time, for the right reason, and in the right way is not easy.* Moreover, the problem of discerning the mean in feelings and actions is made the more difficult because some extremes bear a certain similarity to the mean. Controlled rashness may well resemble courage, which is the mean for rashness. In like manner, a certain degree of prodigality and proper liberality can seem deceptively alike. The problem is made even more puzzling because, from the standpoint of the defect in a feeling or action, the mean can appear to be the extreme. For example, from the standpoint of a coward, a man in the mean, which is courage, will appear rash. To an apathetic person, one who is merely indignant may well appear to be irascible.

Aristotle suggests the following as aids for all who would have their deeds and feelings based on the mean involved:

In all actions and feelings steer clear of the extreme (excess or defect) that is most opposed to the mean for that particular action or feeling.

Note well the extreme to which you are by nature prone and drag yourself in the opposite direction from it.

Guard most of all against any darling pleasures you may be especially attached to, for where such pleasures are concerned you are not an impartial judge.

According to Aristotle, these three suggestions will prove to be signal aids to everyone striving to attain and act on the basis of the mean in his actions and feelings. To lean a little at times toward the extremes can also help one in locating the mean.

Aristotle's discussion of the mean in actions and feelings illustrated for me, when I first read it, what havoc even a wise and practical philosopher can work on a simple subjective injunction by subjecting it to excessive rationality. Such rationality appears to be foreign to the purpose of this precept. The maxim "In nothing too much" was doubtless meant more as a perpetual reminder to individuals of the danger inherent in excess than as a strait jacket designed to produce correct conduct. I have never understood what it is that causes a maxim like this to appear more attractive and meaningful to the generality of people when it is taken in its simple form and at something like face value than when it is hedged about by studied restrictions. But such seems to be the case. It certainly is with me.

But both the simple maxim "In nothing too much" and the doctrine of "the mean" have been anathema to radicals, revolutionaries, and impatient reformers. We know from Thucydides' account of the happenings at Corcyra that moderation—the heart and soul of this maxim and of the doctrine of the mean—was so considered in late fifth century Greece. Thucydides, you will recall, says that "prudent hesitation was branded as specious cowardice, and moderation was declared a cloak for unmanliness. To exhibit an understanding of all situations was [really] an excuse for not acting in any." Sadly, I have heard moderation subjected to exactly the same slanderous interpretation in the last ten years by some "activists." I am afraid that failure to take into account the mean for what is possible and what is not has tricked sincere and well-meaning activists into promising disadvantaged and even disinherited citizens more immediate relief than can possibly be given them immediately. This is too often the natural but no less frustrating and disappointing error of those too impatient to heed the inherent demands of the mean between the possible and the impossible; such an error is almost inevitable when persons cast their thinking in too limited a perspective.

Why did the Greeks put so much emphasis on proportion, proper measure, and balance? I suspect that, like most policies and practices, the concern had its roots in a number of factors. One may have been the close Greek observance of nature, in which they doubtless saw that whatever exceeded its proportional size too much "went the way of all flesh" as being unfitted for survival. One of the more famous dicta of the Greek Stoics was to live according to nature—not according to the wildness, violence, and inconsiderateness of nature, but in accordance with its orderliness, the measured proportion demanded by it in all that it preserves and cooperates with, and in accordance with the limits nature has ordained for healthful human living. Some present-day institutions seem to be seeing that beyond a certain proportional size the law of diminishing returns sets in. So, even though we do not know whether the Greek insistence on balance and proportion in their creations was due in some degree to what they observed in nature, the due measure and proportion in nature were certainly all about them, and, being the shrewd observers that they were, it is not unreasonable to suppose that they were affected by it.

Some cynical commentators have seen in the Greek insistence on balance and proportion an effort at self-discipline to curb an innate Greek tendency to display in conduct just the opposite to due measure and proportion. Certainly some of the Greek political antics—more than one assembly meeting of the Athenians showed more rowdyism than dignity—give legitimate grounds for such an explanation. Thucydides has the Corinthians say (I, 70:9) that the Athenians were so constituted that they could neither rest themselves nor permit others to rest. One can still see signs of this excitability in Greek character any summer evening as the citizens mingle and talk in the city squares of modern Greece, but this explanation appears too superficial for anything as basic and widespread as proportion, due measure, and balance are in almost everything Greek.

The sum and substance of what the Greek maxim "In nothing too much" and Aristotle's doctrine of "the mean," which Horace christened "the golden mean," have meant to me has been this: *They have made me aware that overexcess in actions and feelings leads, more often than not, to undesirable results, while deficiency in actions and feelings generally proves unsatisfactory.* As a result, conduct and feelings based on something like the proper mean and due proportion, considered in sufficient perspective, have for some years seemed to me a *sine qua non* for the best understanding and the most satisfactory solutions to life's more important questions and problems.

XV   A Citizen's Tacit Contract

Plato's classic dialogue concerning a citizen's tacit contract with his government and fellow citizens would seem to constitute a timely addition to these little disquisitions. We read every day of the loose, superficial talk advocating organized disruption and even immobilization of any and all governmental and business functions and practices that displease one segment or another of our society. It seems sad that, despite all the money and effort we have put into education, some citizens apparently do not see or recognize two of the most basic antecedents back of every well-ordered society.

First, they do not or will not see that mankind emerged into effective, civilized life because its members gradually devised and voluntarily submitted and committed themselves to rules and regulations based on the greatest freedom and justice feasible for group living. According to these rules and regulations, each group agreed to acknowledge and respect the rights of every other group. In this new design for community living, every citizen wishing to enjoy the advantages of a more civilized life agreed, at least tacitly, to abide by these newly devised governmental rules and regulations or to seek any changes he might wish in them through the legal means agreed upon and provided for by the community for effecting needed or desired changes. These erstwhile jungle dwellers knew better than to resort to change through force of any kind, unless this new arrangement became functionally intolerable to something like a majority of the citizens. On any other basis, the new society knew it would be on its way back to its former jungle life. For there is no surer or quicker way back to jungle life for any society than for its citizens to feel that they are obligated to obey only such laws as they happen to like, as their ancestors did before emerging from the jungle.

The second antecedent so many of our educated citizens seem wholly unaware of is the inexorable, logical fact that *no citizen's home, family, and possessions can ever be any safer than is his country.* Consequently, every citizen who declines to answer his country's call for help in times of genuine peril is, by that act, removing himself from any part in guaranteeing the safety and protection of his own home and family. This is the ultimate recognition that drives men to respond to such an unwelcome assignment as war, when the choice is between being able to live on one's feet, or being forced to live on one's knees.

Confusion often arises in this matter because many —perhaps most—citizens cannot easily discern when such a choice really threatens until they are eyeball to eyeball with the choice, whereas the more perceptive citizen can perceive it much earlier. But once the citizens realize that whatever threatens their country simultaneously threatens all that is dearest to them personally, only a real derelict will fail to respond. And, as the Platonic Socrates saw, there is no more deadly threat to a country—and therefore to individual citizens—than an active disrespect for and defiance of a country's laws and officers of the law. Moreover, isn't the effort to portray as nonviolent activity the disruption and immobilization of government decisions and business functions *by bodily force* merely a specious rationalization of what is really dishonest double talk? Few things prove more wearisome than the frequent self-righteous implication by such scofflaws of the superiority of their sensitive consciences and their moral sensitivity.

The real problems involved in the question of to what extent a citizen is obligated to keep faith with his responsibility to his country's laws and governmental design, which have enabled him to live a civilized life, confronted Socrates of Athens in the harshest kind of terms in 399 B.C. You will recall that he had been brought to trial in his seventieth year on the vague charge of introducing strange gods and corrupting the Athenian youths—the standard charges brought against honest inquirers in every age. The trial was conducted quite regularly and legally in every way as far as the state was concerned. Yet Socrates, being unpopular with the populace—as most original thinkers are—was condemned to drink hemlock by a vote of 281 out of 501 jurymen.

Normally, Socrates would have been put to death in a day or so. But an ancient religious custom gave him a respite of thirty days. For some centuries, the Athenians had been sending a sacred mission every year to Apollo's shrine on the island of Delos. Athenian law forbade any executions by the state from the time this mission set out until it returned, and storms could sometimes delay their return for quite a while. The delegation for the year 399 B.C. set out on the day after Socrates was condemned and was gone for thirty days. During this time Socrates was kept in prison, where he appears to have been visited frequently by his friends and companions.

The Athenians disposed of citizens they regarded as undesirable by sending them into exile or by executing them. They seem to have been more interested in getting rid of those they considered undesirable than in wreaking punishment or vengeance on them. If a citizen condemned to execution could escape by stealth into some other community willing to receive him, little effort was made to have him extradited.

So, during Socrates' thirty-day respite, his followers did their best to persuade him to allow them to spirit him out of Athens and thus thwart his execution. But they were unsuccessful for several reasons, which Socrates made clear: When he became an Athenian citizen, he agreed to abide by the city's laws and to seek redress from any shortcomings found in them through the designated legal means. Second, the laws of the state were not responsible for the prejudiced judgment of the jurymen, for the trial had been legally correct and there was no legal justification for a new trial. Further, there was no other city that could afford him a social and political climate that would tolerate the inquiries to which he had dedicated his entire active life, and a life deprived of examination into it and its meaning for man was as bad or worse than no life for Socrates. (He had declared at his trial that the unexamined life was not livable for man.) Worst of all, for one who had claimed all his life that the most important thing in life was not mere living but living in a manner fitting and worthy of a human being—for such a one to allow himself to be stealthily sneaked out of Athens, shamefully returning evil for evil on the laws of his land that he might merely continue to live somewhere, was an intolerable prospect for Socrates. Finally, to participate in any such escape would negate everything he had taught in Athens and would neutralize everything he might teach thereafter. Socrates was therefore unwilling to purchase a few more years of living at such a price as that.

Before taking up Socrates' reasons for his decision, a few words about exile in early times—a penalty Socrates could have proposed for himself at the time of his conviction—and about Socrates' outlook and approach to life seem necessary. Modern students are puzzled when they read of ancient persons' preferring death to permanent exile. It is invariably difficult for twentieth-century man to understand how intimately early man was attached to his homeland and to the group with which he felt identified. He felt himself an organic part of the citizenry socially, economically, politically, and religiously; as he participated in all these aspects of the society he was born into, he felt himself a flesh-and-blood participant.

To be forced into permanent exile was like cutting *the umbilical cord*. Instead of being a participating citizen in his native society, he became a wandering spectator in a society with which he was allowed no identity.

All that he really loved was then forbidden to him. He could not become a full-fledged citizen of the group with which he would be living. His property in his native land would be confiscated, and he could hardly inherit any in his new country. He was a rootless wanderer, moving at times from country to country, looked upon as a foreigner and unable to identify satisfactorily anywhere (Shakespeare refers to exile as "speechless death"); further, to be apprehended in his native land meant death. In the light of such ancient feelings and conditions, it is small wonder that men of this time often would prefer death to permanent exile.

To understand Socrates at all, one needs to have some idea of the beliefs he acted upon and of his outlook on life. No specific statement of these has survived, so they must be inferred from various discussions and statements by him. He apparently had an undiscourageable belief that there was back of human life and the universe "a greater power than man could successfully contradict," a power that, as he saw it, was clearly on the side of the greatest possible justice and goodness in human conduct, affairs, and relationships. He refers to this power now in the singular (god) and now in the plural (gods). For Socrates, each man's primary task was to become as just and good a person as he possibly could, regardless of what it might cost him—even if that were his life. In Socrates' judgment, man was endowed with something he called a soul—man's prime self, as well as possession. He therefore considered it man's chief task, in and throughout his entire life, *to make and to keep his soul the very best it could possibly be.*

Socrates always maintained that his continual search for truth and true wisdom, which had constituted his life's work, had been assigned him by the god. "This work I say, men of Athens, has been assigned to me by the god through oracles, dreams, and in every way in which any other divine service has been assigned to men." [20] One would suppose that anyone feeling so about his life's work would show something of a messianic complex, but Socrates showed nothing of the kind. He displayed no urge to save the world or to compel any person to accept the particular ideas he had chosen to live by. Persuade? Yes! Pressure in any way? No! The only idea he seems to have urged on men everywhere was a general one: That they should see to it that their souls became and were kept at their potential best. But just how each person was to achieve that was left to the individual. That Socrates kept his mind and all his perceptive powers entirely open is shown by the fact that he came to the end of his life still searching for truth and true wisdom. The *Euthyphro* dialogue, dated dramatically on the day of Socrates' trial, shows this quite clearly. He remained ever ready to reason out again anything anyone said he didn't understand or disagreed with him in, and he was always ready himself to obey whatever reasoning appeared best to him as he reasoned it out.

Socrates claimed he had had since childhood a divine spirit, a voice that always checked him when he

137

was on the wrong path concerning anything or was about to do something wrong. It remained silent whenever he was planning or was doing what was right or good. Whenever this monitor interrupted him, he always stopped whatever he was planning or about to do. It was this voice that had kept him out of political life. It had served him so well throughout his life that he could believe, after he was convicted, that, since this voice had not bothered him in any aspect of his trial, what had happened to him in this trial was evidently good for him. His warning voice had not bothered him when he left home that morning, nor on his way to the court, nor at any point in his defense, even though it had on former occasions checked him in the middle of what he happened to be doing or discussing. Socrates concluded, therefore, that everything he was experiencing had not happened to him by chance but was within the will of his divine monitor for him. It was possible therefore that it was now best for him to die and be freed from troubles.

So much for Socrates' beliefs and outlook. Let's turn now to the reasons Socrates gave for not allowing his friends to spirit him out of his native Athens. His reasons are given in the Platonic dialogue *Crito*, parts of which I have already discussed in another context.

The dialogue opens, just before dawn, on the day before Socrates is to drink the hemlock, with Socrates sound asleep and Crito sitting silent beside Socrates' bed. Socrates soon wakes up and the dialogue begins. Crito informs Socrates that the boat returning from the sacred mission to Delos is to arrive in Athens on that day. This news means that Socrates will die on the next day. Socrates calmly prophesies, from a dream he has just had, that the boat will not get to Athens for yet another day.

Crito begins to urge Socrates to let himself be persuaded to escape, and he expresses his fear that the multitude will think Socrates has been put to death because his followers, one of whom is Crito himself, were too stingy to put up the money necessary to save him. When Socrates reminds Crito that they had formerly concluded they were not to be concerned with what the multitude thought but only with what the best people might think, Crito says they must consider what the multitude think because, as Socrates' case shows, they can bring the greatest of evils upon a person when their prejudices are aroused. "O that the multitude were able to bring on people the greatest of evils," Socrates replied, "for in that case they might also be able to bring on people the greatest good. But as it is, all they do is just whatever they happen to do."

Crito next resorts to some arguments that sound surprisingly contemporary. But, my dear Socrates, he says, it isn't right for you to give yourself up when you could be saved. You will be doing thereby the very thing your enemies are eager for. Furthermore, you will seem to be deserting your children when you could save yourself and help bring them to manhood. You will seem also to be choosing the easiest way out of your responsibilities. Finally, I'm afraid, Crito says, you will make it appear that this entire affair concerning you has turned out as it has because of cowardice on our and on your part.

Socrates thought that previous discussions had long ago discredited such suggestions as these; yet, true to his regular practice, he feels he must go through the arguments against them again to show once more their speciousness. He therefore sets out to prove dialectically the following: (1) That the opinions of the *hoi polloi* are untrustworthy criteria whenever and wherever the search for truth is concerned; only the opinions of the one who knows—truth itself—must be followed in that search, if our first purpose in life is to be not mere living but living well *i.e.*, honorably and justly. (2) That to act unjustly happens to be in any and all situations both an evil and a shameful thing for the one acting unjustly. (3) That one must never treat anyone unjustly, nor wrong in turn one who has wronged him, no matter to what extent the person has wronged him. *For it can never be right to do wrong.* (4) That one must carry out, free from all deceit, whatever just agreement one has made with another.

Crito assents again to Socrates' proofs in all these matters. The next thing to do is to apply them to the following questions: (1) Will it be just for Socrates to be sneaked out of the city as Crito is suggesting? (2) Will Socrates be breaking the agreement he made with the city when he became a citizen? (3) Will he be wronging Athens in turn for the wrong she has done to him? (4) And finally, Will he be wronging those whom least of all he should wrong—the laws of the city through which he had been able to live in a civilized society? The answers to all these questions are cast in the form of an imaginary dialogue between Socrates and the laws of Athens. Let us be sure to note and to remember that the laws discussed in this dialogue are those general and widely employed laws that are basic to any enlightened and civilized life—those pertaining to marriage, family, and education. This dialogue is not concerned with those more superficial laws—those connected with stopgap decrees, legislative mandates, or mere safety measures such as speed limits and the like.

The imaginary dialogue, which now follows between Socrates and the laws supporting civilized life in Athens, is so basic to the arguments involved that I am afraid that a mere outline or paraphrase would leave unclear the matters involved. So I shall merely translate the rest of the *Crito* (50ab) and thus permit any reader to decide for himself on the validity of its answers to the questions listed above. One should remember that this dialogue took place some 2400 years ago, in the light of the problems and knowledge of that time and not on the basis of present-day knowledge and situations.

SOCRATES TO CRITO.
Suppose that as we are about to sneak out (or however our action should be described) of Athens, the laws, the guardians of the common good of the city, should accost us and say: "Tell us, Socrates, what are you intending to do? Aren't you planning, by this deed you are considering, to destroy us, the laws, and the entire city, as far as you are concerned? Or do you think any city can continue to exist and not

be overthrown in which decisions legally reached by its courts are nullified and wholly disregarded by private citizens?"

What shall we answer to these and similar questions, Crito? For anyone, and especially a professional orator, could make quite a defense in behalf of the law that is being destroyed by our act —the law which enjoins that decisions reached by the courts shall be valid and binding. Or shall we reply that the court did not decide our case rightly? Or what shall we say?

CRITO.

Just that, by Zeus, Socrates.

SOCRATES.

But what if the laws should say: "Is that what was agreed to between you and us, or was it that you would abide by whatever decisions the city would legally render through its courts?" If I should wonder at their saying this, they would doubtless say: "Socrates, don't wonder at what we are saying, but, since you are accustomed to use the question and answer method, answer our questions.

"What do you have against the state and us that is causing you to be planning to destroy us? Was it not we who first gave you civilized existence, since it was through us that your father married your mother and became your lawful father? Tell us, therefore, do you hold that our laws concerned with marriage are not good laws?"

"I find no fault with them," I would say.

[The Laws]. "Well, what about the laws concerned with the nurture and education of children in which you were educated? Did not such of us as were

enacted for that purpose do well in requiring your
father to have you educated in music and gymnastics?"
[*Note:* Music covered all subjects confined to mental
activity and gymnastics covered all that pertained
to bodily accomplishments.]

I would say they did well in requiring such.

[The Laws]. "Very well then. Since you were
begotten, nourished, and educated by us, can you deny,
first of all, that both you and your forebears have
from birth been our offspring and servants? And if
this is so, do you think it right for the relationship
between you and us to be that of equals, so that you
think it just for you to do in turn to us whatever we
undertake to do to you? You surely never considered
yourself to be on equal terms before the law with
your father—or your master, if you happened to have
one—which gave you the right to do to them whatever
they did to you. If you were abusively addressed by
them, you did not speak abusively to them in turn,
did you? Or, being struck, you did not strike them
in turn, or return like for like in other similar
treatment, did you? Can it be then that you now
suppose yourself to be on equal terms before the law
with your native land and with us, its laws, so that, if
we try to destroy you, thinking it is right for us to do
so, you will try, as far as you can, to destroy us in turn,
and will dare to say, while doing so, that you are
acting justly—you who truly care for the highest
human excellence?

"Or have you become so wise as to forget that your
native land is something holier, more to be revered
and more to be honored than your mother and father
and all your ancestors, and that it holds the greatest

place of honor in the sight of the gods and of men of knowledge and understanding? Have you forgotten therefore (1) That your native country must be revered and yielded to; and that she, rather than your father, must be appeased when she is angry? (2) Or that you must do whatever she bids you to do, or persuade her to a different course, as well as suffer, without protest, if she orders you to suffer? (3) Or that if she shall order you to be imprisoned or beaten or led into war to be wounded or slain, you must do all this—and justly so—and you must neither yield to an enemy nor retreat before him nor leave your post of duty, but both in war, in the courts and everywhere you must do whatever the city and your native land orders you to do, or persuade her what the just course of action is, remembering that, whereas it is an impious thing to employ force against your parents, it is even more impious to resort to force against your native land?"

What shall we answer to these questions, Crito? That the laws are right, or that they are not?

CRITO.

They seem to be right.

SOCRATES.

The laws would perhaps say, "Consider therefore, Socrates, whether we are right in saying that it is not just for you to attempt to do to us what you are attempting to do. For after begetting you into civilized life, then rearing you and providing an education for you, as well as sharing with you and the other citizens all the good things in our power, we also proclaimed, by providing the opportunity to every Athenian wishing it when he comes up to be examined for citizenship and has observed the affairs of the state and us the laws, that anyone to whom we are not pleasing may take his possessions and go wherever he wishes. If we and the city are not pleasing to any Athenian, no one of us stands in his way or forbids his going to live in one of the colonies, or taking his possessions and going to live as a foreigner in any country he wishes to. But whoever chooses to remain here, after he has observed the manner in which our court decisions are reached and how the other affairs of the city are conducted, we claim that from then on he has agreed, by his choice, to abide by whatever we may order him to do.

"And we say that whoever disobeys us is unjust on three counts: (1) because he disobeys those who gave him civilized existence; (2) because he disobeys those who nourished and brought him up; (3) because, after agreeing to obey us, he neither obeys us nor persuades us wherein we are wrong—even though we gave him that alternative and did not harshly command him to do whatever we might order but allowed him one of the two courses of action: to persuade us, or do what we say—neither of which he does.

"Moreover, Socrates, if you shall do what you now have in mind, we say you will make yourself liable to these charges to the greatest degree possible— more so than any other Athenian."

If then I should ask why? they would perhaps tauntingly say: "Because you happen to have entered into this agreement to a greater extent than any other Athenian." For they would say:

"We have strong proofs, Socrates, that both we

and the city are pleasing to you; for you would not have stayed in the city more consistently than any other Athenian, unless it was especially pleasing to you. You never went on any of the sacred missions sent by the city (except once to the Isthmus), nor did you go anywhere else, unless it was to go on a military expedition to some place. Nor did you ever go on journeys as other men did. You had no desire to get acquainted with any other state and its laws, but we and our city were quite sufficient for you. To such an extent did you choose and agree to be governed as we might command! You begat children and carried on other activities here on the ground that you were well pleased with the city.

"Moreover, it was possible for you to have proposed exile for yourself, if you had preferred it, and you could then have done, with the city's blessing, what you are now attempting to do against its will. But you prided yourself then on not being vexed if it should become necessary for you to die, and you chose death, as you said, to exile. Now, however, you neither feel ashamed as you confront these words nor show any reverence for us, the laws, since you are trying to destroy us; and you are doing what the lowest slave would do—trying to run away contrary to our compacts and agreements with you, according to which you consented to be governed by us. So answer first for us this particular question: When we say that you have agreed by your conduct, and not just by words, that you would be governed as we might demand, are we speaking the truth or are we not?"

What shall we answer to this question, Crito?

Anything other than that we agree?

CRITO.

We must agree, Socrates.

SOCRATES.

Won't the laws then say, "Are you doing anything else, Socrates, than breaking your covenant and agreement with us, although you were neither coerced nor tricked into making them, nor were you compelled to decide about them in any short time? You had seventy years in which it was possible for you to leave the city, if we were not pleasing to you, and if the agreements made with us appeared unjust to you at any time. But you chose neither Lacedaemon nor Crete which you were always saying had excellent laws, nor did you choose any other city of the Greeks or barbarians, but you left Athens less frequently than the blind, the lame, and other cripples. So much more were you pleased with the city and with us the laws than the rest of the Athenians were! And who could be pleased with a city that had no laws? Are you not going to abide by your agreements now? You will if you are willing to obey us, Socrates. And you will not make yourself an object of ridicule by escaping from the city. [The laws now begin to answer Crito's earlier reasons why Socrates must not stay in Athens and be executed.]

"Consider moreover what a fine favor you will be conferring on yourself and these friends of yours by violating these agreements and failing to live up to them. For it is practically certain that your friends will be in danger of being exiled and thus deprived of their city, in addition to having their property confiscated.

"As for yourself, if you shall flee into any of the nearest cities—into Megara or Thebes, both of which are governed by excellent laws—you will enter, Socrates, as an enemy of their government, and all who care for their city will look askance at you, regarding you as a destroyer of laws. By this act of yours, you will so confirm the decision of the jurymen that they will seem to have decided your case rightly. For whoever proves to be a destroyer of laws would doubtless seem to be a corruptor of young and thoughtless men.

"What then will you do? Avoid the best governed cities and the most law-abiding men? And if you do that, will life be worth living for you? Or will you approach these well-governed people and have the effrontery to try to reason out with them—what moral problems, pray, Socrates? The ones you have long been discussing here: that virtue and justice, together with laws and lawful procedures, are the things of most worth and importance to men? Don't you think that such conduct on the part of Socrates will appear most unseemly? You are obliged to think so

"Or will you stay clear of these orderly places and go to Crito's friends in Thessaly, where the greatest disorder and licentiousness flourish? They would perhaps gladly listen to you as you described the ridiculous plight in which you escaped from prison, after changing your appearance by throwing around you some contrived garment or skin of an animal or some of the other disguises runaways are accustomed to escape in.

"And will no one remark upon the fact that you,

an old man, with little of life in all likelihood left to you, dared so shamefully to cling to the desire to continue living that you violated the greatest of laws? Perhaps not, unless you offend someone.

Otherwise, you will hear many things said about you, Socrates, of which you are as yet unworthy. Moreover, you will pass the rest of your life cringing like a slave before all men. And what will you do in Thessaly besides feast, as though you had run away for banquets in Thessaly? And what will become of those discussions of yours about justice and other virtues?

"And is it your children you want to live for, so that you may rear and educate them? Will you take them into Thessaly to rear and educate them there, bestowing on them the fine benefit of being made aliens to their native land? Or if you don't take them with you, will they, being reared here in Athens, be any better reared and educated merely because you are alive somewhere, with no opportunity for companionship with them? Your friends will care for them, of course. Well, will they care for them, if you depart for Thessaly, but not care for them, if you depart for Hades? If there is any worth in those who claim to be your friends, you must know they will still care for them.

"Therefore, obey us, Socrates, the ones who nourished you into civilized life and don't consider children or life or anything else of more importance than living justly; so that, when you enter the halls of Hades, you may have these arguments to offer in your defense before those who rule there; since neither for you nor for any of your friends does it appear to be better, holier, or more just for you to do what you are now considering. Nor will it be better for you when you arrive in Hades. As it is, you are departing this life, if depart it you must, wronged not by us, the laws, but by men. But, if you shall escape from Athens in the fashion being proposed, shamefully returning injustice for injustice and repaying evil with evil, having broken your compacts and agreements with us and having wronged those whom least of all you should wrong—yourself, your friends, your native land, and us, the laws—we will be angry with you while you are alive, and our brothers, the laws in Hades, will not receive you kindly when you arrive there; for they will know that you did all you could in an effort to destroy us. So don't let Crito persuade you to do what he suggests, but do instead what we say."

Know you well, my dear Crito, that these are the words I seem to hear, just as the priests of Cybele think they catch the sounds of flutes; and the sound of these words keeps booming away within me, making it impossible for me to hear any others. Know also, therefore, that, if you shall now advance arguments contrary to these which now seem right to me, you will speak in vain. Yet if you think you can accomplish anything by speaking, say on.

CRITO.

I have nothing more to say, Socrates.

SOCRATES.

Then cease your pleading, Crito, and let us fare along this path, since God along this path is leading.

XVI *The Death of Socrates*

Around the turn of the century, before the study of comparative religions was known or regarded seriously in our region, I was taught that only Christians—and genuine Christians at that—could meet death calmly and even serenely, free from every fear. One can easily imagine, therefore, what a surprise it was to me when, at about age twenty-five, I was confronted with Plato's detailed description of Socrates' death, 399 years before the Christian Era. Here was a recorded eye-witness account, bearing all the marks of authenticity, of one who demonstrated as full and as adequate calm, devoid of every fear, when face to face with death and all its fictive terrors, as any Christian martyr ever exemplified.

The discovery of such a discrepancy between what was really true and what I had been taught to believe was documentable fact would simply be brushed aside by most students today. But for me it was a comforting surprise. It was comforting because it verified what I had been suspecting for some time—that what I had been taught in this matter was more propaganda than truth. And one of the greatest pleasures that has come to me from the moderate amount of learning I have been introduced to has been in having many of the erroneous notions held by me exposed for what they were—unmitigated errors.

Unless one reads the account of Socrates' death, it would be difficult to comprehend how completely unperturbed he was and how fully adequate he was for every situation the experience of dying, which he had known was confronting him, could offer. I covet for everyone the experience of reading (or rereading) it at first hand. I have decided, therefore, to translate it for you so that you may know it as nearly as possible at first hand and can make your own evaluation of it.

On the day of Socrates' death, he spent the morning discussing with his special friends his reasons for believing in the immortality of the human soul. What he is said to have said on the subject has been preserved in Plato's dialogue *Phaedo*.

When the discussion was over, Socrates left his friends to take a bath, after which he spent *much* time with his family—we are not told how much time. He later sent them away, because he had heard that wailing at the time of death was a bad omen, and then returned to his friends. It was now getting late in the afternoon, and Socrates was to drink the hemlock at sunset—the regular time for executions.

The details of Socrates' death, as reported to Echecrates in Plato's *Phaedo*, are too vivid and unusual to be paraphrased. I shall merely translate the account of his death as accurately and as objectively as I can, beginning with section 115b of the *Phaedo*. (Phaedo himself is the narrator of this dialogue.)

When Socrates had said all this, Crito said: "Very well, Socrates! But do you have any instructions to give either these friends here or me concerning the children or anything else in the carrying out of which we would please you most?"

"Nothing new, Crito," Socrates replied, "only what I am always saying: that if you will care for yourselves, how you shall be as good as possible, you will be doing me, mine and yourselves a favor, no matter what you do, even if you now make no promises about it. But if you shall fail to care thus for yourselves and shall not be willing to live by the conclusions reached formerly, and again just now, as your guide, nothing you do will amount to anything, no matter how many promises you may now make about it."

[*Note:* This is no self-centered individualism on Socrates' part. He held that the prime prerequisite for being a good citizen and neighbor was to be a good person. And one became a good person by "caring for his soul first of all and seeing to it that it became as good as possible." For from a good self, good flowed out to all it came in contact with.]

"We shall eagerly do this," said Crito, "but how shall we bury you?"

"Any way you wish, if you can catch me and I do not elude you." And with a quiet chuckle he looked toward us and said: "I haven't persuaded Crito, men, that I, the one here who is now guiding and directing each step of the dialogue, am the real Socrates. He thinks I am that one whom he will presently see as a corpse, and is asking how he shall bury *me*. The long discourse I made a while ago intending to encourage both you and myself, saying that when I had drunk the poison *I* would no longer

be present here but would be gone to some
blessedness of the blessed, seems to have been lost on
Crito. You therefore now become bondsmen for me to
Crito," he said—"an opposite bond to that which
he offered to the jurymen for me. His bond was to
assure them that I would remain in Athens. But
you be bondsmen to him that, when I have died, I
will not remain here but will be gone hence. Do this
so that Crito may bear it more easily and will not
be grieved for me, when he sees my body being
buried or cremated, on the ground that *I* am suffering
something terrible, and that he may not say at the
funeral rites that he is laying out or carrying to the
grave or burying Socrates.
[To Crito] For know you well, my dear Crito, that
not to think rightly about a thing not only puts
one into a false relationship with the thing itself but
it works also some evil in one's soul. So you must be
of good courage and say that you are burying my body,
and you must bury it in whatever way it pleases
you and in whatever way you think best accords
with custom."

When he had said this, he stood up and went into
a room to bathe himself. Crito followed him but
urged us to wait where we were. As we waited, we
talked over among ourselves what had been discussed,
examining it again and speaking at times about
how great a disaster had befallen us, absolutely
certain that we would pass the rest of our lives as
though we were orphans deprived of our father.

When he had bathed and the children had been
brought to him—he had two small sons and one

about grown—and the women of the household had come, after he had conversed with them and given, in the presence of Crito, such instructions as he wished, he ordered the women and children to be sent away, and he returned to us.

It was already near sunset; for he had spent *much time inside* [italics mine] with the women of his household and the children. When he came in, after being bathed, he sat down and not much was said afterwards, until the servant of the Eleven [magistrates] came and, standing near Socrates, said: "Socrates, I don't bring against you the charges I generally have to bring against other prisoners; for they become angry and curse me whenever I, compelled by the archons, announce to them that it is time for them to drink the hemlock. But in the time you have been here I have come to know that you are quite different, being, in fact, the noblest, mildest, and best man that has ever come hither; and especially do I know well that you are not now angry with me but with those responsible—you know who they are. Now— for you know what I have come to announce— farewell, and try to bear what is inevitable as easily as possible." Then bursting into tears, he turned and left the room.

And Socrates, looking up at him, said: "And fare- well to you; we will do as you say." At the same time he turned to us and said: "What a considerate and kindly man he is! Throughout the entire time I have been here, he has visited me and at times conversed with me. He was the best kind of fellow, and now how nobly he weeps for me! But come,

Crito: let us obey him! And let someone bring the hemlock, if it has been prepared. And if it hasn't, let someone prepare it."

But Crito said: "I think the sun is still on the mountains, Socrates, and has not yet set. I know also that others have drunk the poison quite a long while after they had been ordered to drink it—after they had eaten and drunk well indeed, and some even after they had enjoyed intimate relationships with whomever they happened to desire. So don't be in a hurry; for there is still time left."

Socrates replied: "Those men you speak of, Crito, quite naturally do as you have said; for they think they gain something thereby. But I will naturally do none of these things; for I think there is nothing to be gained by drinking the poison a little later, except to make myself ridiculous in my own judgment by clinging so to life and trying so to preserve it when none any longer remains. So come," he said, "and obey me; and don't do otherwise."

Upon his saying this, Crito nodded to his attendant who was standing close by. The attendant went out and, after some delay, returned bringing with him the one who was to give the drug, having with him the drug prepared in a cup. When Socrates saw the man, he said: "Very well, my excellent sir,—for you know about these drugs—what must I do?" "Nothing at all," he said, "except drink it and walk around until you feel a heaviness in your legs and then lie down face up. When you have done that the drug will do the rest." At the same time he handed the cup to Socrates. He took the cup, even quite cheerfully, Echecrates, without the slightest trembling or change in his color or countenance, but looking steadfastly at the man as his custom was, with his head tilted down like an angry bull's, he asked the man: "What do you say about pouring a libation to someone from this drink? Is it possible or not?" "We mix only as much," he said, "as we consider the proper amount to drink." "I understand," Socrates said; "but it is both possible and right to pray to the gods that this journey from here there may be a fortunate one. All of which I do pray and may it so be."

When he had said this, he readily and cheerfully lifted the cup to his lips and drained its entire contents. Up until then most of us had been able to keep our tears back reasonably well. But when we saw him drinking and continuing to drink until he had drained the entire draught, we could no longer restrain ourselves, and, in spite of myself, the tears came streaming down, so that I covered my head and wept, not for that one but for myself and my sad fate in that I would be deprived henceforward of such a comrade. And Crito, even sooner than I, got up and went out when he was unable to keep back his tears. Apollodorus who even before this had never ceased weeping then broke into such weeping and wailing that he broke down every one present, except Socrates himself, who exclaimed, "What on earth are you doing, my strange and wonderful friends? This was my chief reason for sending the women away—that we might have no such unseemly conduct; for I have heard that one should die amid good omens. So keep quiet and bear up with a strong heart." When we heard that, we became quiet and checked our weeping.

After walking around, when he said his legs were getting heavy, he lay down face up, as the executioner had ordered him. The man who had given him the drug began feeling and examining his feet and legs at intervals. And finally, pressing very hard on his foot, he asked him if he felt it. Socrates said no. After this he later pressed the lower part of his legs, and, going on up his body in this fashion, he showed us that he was growing cold and stiff. The man, touching himself, said that when it reached his heart, he would then be gone. When the coldness was already just about up to the lower part of his abdomen, Socrates uncovered himself—his face had been covered—and said what was his last utterance: "Crito," he said, "we owe a cock to Asclepius. Don't neglect to pay it." "We will do that," said Crito. "See if you have anything else to say." He made no answer to Crito's question, but after a short time a shudder ran through his body, and, when the man who administered the drug uncovered his face, his eyes were set. When Crito saw this, he closed his mouth and eyelids.

That was the end, Echecrates, of our comrade, the best, the wisest and most just, we would say, of all the men of his time that we ever knew in our experience.

Thus, according to Plato, did Socrates, the son of Sophroniscus, pass from this veiled and limited existence to what he called the region of the blessed, feeling no rancor or ill against either his accusers or those who had condemned him. The manner of his death accorded well with all that is known of his life and his lifelong professions. He was the most profound spiritual genius that Greece ever produced, and is easily reckoned among the greatest spiritual geniuses of all time. No person, so far as I know, ever tried more diligently or consistently than Socrates did to discover, as best he could, the primary purpose the Creator must have had in mind for His human creatures and, having found it, to do it, as best he could discern it, no matter what the cost. He has therefore long seemed to me the most outstanding pre-Christian "Christian" of whom we have record. For the Gospels make it rather clear that the real Christian is the person who regards it as his primary task in life to discover, as best he can, the will of the Father Creator and then do it the best he can, let it cost him whatever it will. If this was Jesus' test of a true follower, as he said numerous times, then I know of no one who has better qualified himself to be considered a follower than Socrates of Athens, as both his life and death show. Such a statement may shock the orthodox. If it does, it is to be hoped that they will remember, as history shows, that it is not from the orthodox alone that true religion or Christianity is to be learned.

Because of the calmness and even willingness with which Socrates met his death, some precipitous readers have accused him, as they have also accused Jesus of Nazareth, of suffering from a martyr complex. They do this in spite of the fact that a consideration of the total facts, as far as they are known, make such a conclusion untenable, as I see it. For neither Socrates nor Jesus of Nazareth "willed" their deaths until after they had voluntarily *acquiesced* in their deaths, if necessary, rather than fail to keep faith with what they had irrevocably committed their full lives to.

Socrates had made an irrevocable commitment early in life to the prime task of keeping his soul as good a soul as possible and as free as possible from all injustice and wrong-doing at any and all cost. "All cost" would include death, of course; but the full evidence available portrays Socrates as preferring to live, *if* he could do so without breaking faith with the voluntary commitment to which he had irrevocably committed his life. Socrates told Crito that he was willing to be sneaked out of Athens, *if* he could be shown that it was right and just for him to do so. He even went through a re-examination of his dilemma to see if it would prove to be right and free of all wrong-doing for him to escape, contrary to the contract he had made with Athens when, at the age of twenty, he took the oath of citizenship. When it turned out that the dilemma would not allow him to escape without betraying his irrevocable commitment and all he had taught and stood for, Socrates, rather than willing or wishing his death, only *acquiesced* in it voluntarily, as the dilemma compelled him to.

In like manner, Jesus of Nazareth showed by his disturbed feelings and earnest plea to his Father in the Garden of Gethsemane that he was not seeking death. "Father," he said (Luke 22:42), "if it accords with your will, take this cup from me; yet let not my will but yours be done." He too had made an irrevocable commitment

160

earlier in life to do what he considered to be his Father's will, no matter what the cost. The dilemma that was closing in on him in Gethsemane left him only one of two choices, just as Socrates' dilemma had: to live and betray thereby his irrevocable commitment to his Father, or to keep faith with it and die. He thereupon *acquiesced* in his death, not because he wished or willed it, but because he had to, if he was not to prove unfaithful to his unqualified commitment to the doing of his Father's will at all costs. It was only after this voluntary *acquiescence* in his death that Jesus could say, without appearing to want to renege on his solemn promise, "No one has taken my life from me; but I lay it down of my own accord."

All this is neither to say nor imply that Socrates is to be compared with Jesus of Nazareth. There are several striking similarities in their experience, their attitudes, and their purposes. But there are neither enough of these nor are they of a kind that would constitute a legitimate comparison. The history and effect of each one on his followers and on succeeding generations are enough to negate any real comparison. I have to say, however, that I have found it helpful to keep in mind their several remarkable similarities and at the same time their wide and compelling differences. This has proved for me a much more rewarding approach to both men than the attitude that refuses to admit that there are any legitimate similarities between Jesus of Nazareth and any person living at his time or before it.

XVII Hail and Farewell

Some of the most striking and rewarding insights to be found in Greek literature are contained in the "philosophical" tidbits one encounters in Greek epigrams. These are very short poems, frequently just two lines long, yet they often have in them surprising words of wisdom, highly valuable for constructive and adventurous living, if the suggestions in them are heeded. Gravestone epitaphs, frequently only a two-line couplet, often contain such insights and wisdom.

The following epitaph, apparently erected on a seashore at or near the place where a sailor was wrecked and drowned, will illustrate this. It is attributed to the Sicilian poet Theodoridas, a writer of various kinds of epitaphs, who flourished in the latter half of the third century B.C. The epitaph is as follows:

I am the tomb of a shipwreck; but you sail on;
When we went down, the other ships weathered the storm.

Here we have the old Greek restless adventuresomeness and their insatiable desire to learn and know, still asserting itself even as late as the third century B.C. We first meet this insatiable desire in Odysseus, the hero of the *Odyssey*. The Romans called him Ulixes, which later writers changed to Ulysses.

This aspect of Greek character was later amplified

by Dante in Canto XXVI of his *Inferno,* where he portrays Ulysses as declaring that neither his fondness for his son, nor pity for his old father, nor his love for Penelope—all of which should have made him happy—could overcome his insatiable desire to gain experience and knowledge of the vices and the worth of men. Consequently, Ulysses (Odysseus), according to Dante, assembled some of his old Ithacan comrades and set out again, resolved to "sail beyond the sunset and the baths of all the western stars" (to use Tennyson's phrasing). He thus sailed past Gibraltar and into the Atlantic until he came to an unspecified country where he with all his comrades and ship were destroyed.

Tennyson took this idea of a Ulysses who could not give up his restless urge to see and know, even after ten years of fighting around Troy plus ten years of wandering, and wove it into a poem of seventy lines called *Ulysses.* It was first published in 1842, and still remains one of the most inspiring short poems in the English language. This poem will amply repay looking up and reading—even rereading. For no one has better caught and expressed the dominant feeling of the Hellenic people at their best, which held that it was "never too late to seek a newer world," and also their sovereign passion "to strive, to seek, to find, and not to yield."

Notes

1. Edwin Markham, *Poems of Edwin Markham*, selected and arranged by Charles L. Wallis (New York, Harper & Brothers, 1950), 5.

2. *The House of Atreus: Being the* Agamemnon, *the* Libation-Bearers, *and the* Eumenides *of Aeschylus*, trans. by E. D. A. Morshead (London, Kegan Paul & Co., 1881).

3. William Shakespeare, *The Tragedie of Antonie and Cleopatra*, Charlotte Porter and Helen A. Clarke, eds. (Windsor edition; New York, Thomas Y. Crowell Co., 1903 and 1908).

4. The only source I have for this is a newspaper clipping from a small syndicated work called "Sentence Sermons."

5. This quotation was taken from Sir Winston Churchill's radio address, which I heard and later checked with the reports of the address in the news media.

6. Paul Geren, *Burma Diary* (New York, Harper & Brothers, 1943), 50, 58.

7. This is my own definition, as I have tried to suggest in the text.

8. Ronald Bridges and Luther A. Weigle, *The Bible Word Book* (New York, Thomas Nelson & Sons, 1960), 210.

9. Plato, *The Symposium*, trans. by W. Hamilton (Penguin Classics, L 24; Baltimore, Penguin Books, Inc., 1951), 79–95.

10. Sir R. W. Livingstone, *Greek Ideals and Modern Life* (Cambridge, Harvard University Press, 1935), 154.

11. Plato, *Gorgias*, Gonzalez Lodge, ed. (College Series of Greek Authors; Boston, Ginn & Co., 1896).

12. I translated this passage for use in the revised edition of *Greek Literature in Translation*, George Howe and Gustave

Adolphus Harrar, eds. (New York, Harper & Brothers, 1948).
Used by permission of Harper & Row, New York.

13. David Grene, *Man in His Pride* (Chicago; The University of Chicago Press, 1950).

14. William Shakespeare, *Measure for Measure*, Charlotte Porter and Helen A. Clarke, eds. (Windsor edition; New York, Thomas Y. Crowell Co., 1903 and 1908).

15. Eliza Gregory Wilkins, *The Delphic Maxims in Literature* (Chicago, The University of Chicago Press, 1929).

16. Herbert J. Muller, *The Uses of the Past* (Oxford; Oxford University Press, 1952), 70.

17. Wilkins, *Delphic Maxims*.

18. My translation of Aristotle, *The Nicomachean Ethics*, II, vi, sec. 11.

19. *Ibid.*, II, vi, 15.

20. My translation of Plato, *The Apology of Socrates*, 330c4.